The Lost Gods of England

The Lost Gods of
England

Brian Branston

with 124 illustrations, 19 in colour

Book Club Associates London

To
HUGH BARRETT *farmer*
and
FRED STREETER *gardener*

This edition published 1974 by
Book Club Associates
by arrangement with Thames and Hudson Ltd

© Thames and Hudson Ltd, London 1957
First published 1957
This edition © Thames and Hudson Ltd, London 1974
Printed in Great Britain by Jarrold and Sons Ltd, Norwich

CONTENTS

Chapter One

WAYLAND'S BONES

Locked away in my desk I have a stump of human bone almost fifteen hundred years old. As far as I can judge, it is a fragment of one of the thin ridged bones of the forearm of a man. On the surface it is discoloured, dull and hair-cracked with age. It crumbles at the ends if you don't handle it carefully. The pipe where the living marrow once lay is now filled with a gritty, sandy peat, for this remnant of an ancient skeleton came from a grave mound on Snape Common near Aldeburgh in 12 Suffolk. From this 'low' or barrow there was brought to light in 1862 the first of the only three English ship-burials known at present. These interments date from Anglo-Saxon times and the Snape Common burial probably took place not much more than fifty years after the Angles, Saxons and Jutes first invaded Britain; that is to say, the mound was raised about AD 500. My stump of bone was once part of the living body of a man, a chief or prince of the Angle race who was important enough to have been buried not merely in a hole but lying in the boat which was to take him 'who drew from out the boundless deep' to the kingdom of the dead.

It is perhaps idle now to speculate on who or what he was: though such speculations have always teased people's imagination. One of this man's early descendants was asking like questions a thousand years ago:

> Where now are the bones
>   of Wayland the wise,
> that goldsmith
>   so glorious of yore . . . ?
>
> Who now wots of the bones
>   of Wayland the wise
> or which is the low
>   where they lie?

These two stanzas were translated from Latin into Anglo-Saxon over a millennium ago, and when the translator posed his rhetorical questions neither he nor his listeners could have supplied an answer, for Wayland Smith was no creature of flesh and blood but a personage from an ancient mythology which the Christian Church had done its utmost to suppress, the mythology of our forefathers. Nevertheless, Wayland went underground otherwise than suggested by the poet, for his memory was preserved on the lips of the ordinary folk of England. They were mindful of him in their oral tales as the supreme smith of the gods even after his name had been rubbed out of Christian writings. Just as they knew their own family trees by heart for generations back, since before their arrival in England even, so they recalled Wayland's lineage. His pedigree would be as familiar to them as their own, they would know his son was Widia, and his father Wada; and that with his child on his shoulder Wayland strode through water nine yards deep. This was remembered in folklore, this was matter for popular song in spite of the passage of centuries, the ban of the Church and the melting-pot of the Norman Conquest, as we gather when Chaucer relates of his heroine and her uncle in *Troilus and Criseyde* how

he songe, she playede, he told a tale of Wade

– Wade being, of course, Wada the father of Wayland.
Wayland Smith was a personage known as intimately to our Anglo-Saxon forebears as say Robin Hood is known to us. The mention of his name was enough to call up the stories attached to it without their ever needing to be told. Because of their familiarity with him on the one hand and the enmity of the Church towards paganism on the other, the references in writing to Wayland that remain are distinctly offhand. Nevertheless, there *are* written references to him, which is more than can be said of some personages in the Old English mythology who were far more important than Wayland. Our oldest epic poem *Beowulf* recalls the fabulous smith and so does another scrap of Anglo-Saxon verse named after its hero, *Waldere*. In the one case Wayland is mentioned as the artificer of a superb war-coat and in the other of an unsurpassable sword. But the oldest extant Anglo-Saxon lyric poem *Deor's Lament* hints, and little more than hints, at the wild tale by which Wayland was remembered among the Norse peoples and (under another name) by the Greeks. *Deor's Lament* opens with the following lines:

> Wayland the steadfast warrior knew what it meant to be banished; he suffered miserably; his only messmates sorrow and heartache and exile in the wintry cold. This was after Nidhad had prisoned and pined him, had bound with supple sinew bonds a far better man.
> But that passed off; so may this.
> Beadohild's brother's death did not crush her spirit so much as did her own wretched condition when she knew she was heavy with child. Never afterwards did she rejoice for thought of what should befall.
> But that passed off and so may this. . . .

This allusive style tells us very little except that the audience for whom the poem was intended already knew the story of Wayland off by heart: how many more such stories for which not even allusions remain have been lost? We should not know that Beadohild and her pregnancy were connected with Wayland even, had not the tale been written down and preserved in Norse manuscripts: nor should we know how or why her brother died nor at whose hand.

A more graphic reminder of Wayland Smith is to be found carved on the front panel of the celebrated walrus-ivory box known as the Franks Casket now in the British Museum. This excellent piece of seventh-century north of England craftsmanship was rescued from oblivion by Sir A. W. Franks who gave this account of his acquisition in a letter dated 10 March, 1867:

> When the casket came into my hands, it was in pieces. It was obtained from a dealer in Paris, and was considered to be Scandinavian. The form however of the runes [round the edges of the box] clearly proved its origin. I traced the casket into the hands of Professor Mathieu of Clermont-Ferrand in Auvergne, who gave me the following account of it: *This monument of the past came to light in a middle-class home in Auzon, the market-town of a canton in the Brionde district, Haute-Loire county. The ladies of the farmhouse had used it as a work-box for their needles and cottons. At that time it had silver mountings but one of the sons of the household stripped them off and swopped them for a ring of the kind we call* chevalières. . . . I should add that Professor Mathieu informed me, that in consequence of the removal of the mountings the box fell to pieces and some of them got lost. He offered a reward for the missing end, but it was supposed to have been thrown away on a heap, and carried out to manure vines!

As a matter of fact, we now know that the missing panel of the Franks Casket was never lost. It appears that Professor Mathieu did in truth sell all the pieces to a M. Carrand, a Paris dealer, in 1857 without knowing it. At the time Franks wrote to him, the Professor, looking back on the deal, seems to have believed that he sold the box to Carrand with one side missing. Franks paid a high price to Carrand for all the pieces but one, which Franks was later given to understand had been lost in the way Professor Mathieu described. However, when the dealer Carrand died he bequeathed the missing side of the casket to the Bargello in Florence where it remains to this day.

The Franks Casket is important to us because it depicts scenes from Anglo-Saxon pagan myth alongside others from Classical myth and Bible story: its front panel shows Wayland the Smith (without caption – his story being presumably so well known) sharing space with a Biblical scene, the presentation of gifts to Christ by the three Wise Men (but this scene – perhaps not so readily recognized at that time by the new Christians, is titled in runes MFXI 'Magi'). The Wayland scene is a composite one depicting two episodes from his story: on the left Wayland is working over the anvil in his smithy. He wears a shortish kilt which has allowed the carver to show that there is some deformity about the smith's legs. At his feet lies a headless body. In his left hand he grasps a pair of tongs gripping a human head. His right hand is outstretched to meet the left hand of one of the two female figures who are facing him. So much for the first scene; in the second, on the right of the Wayland panel, there is a single human figure, a woman to judge by the flowing drapery and lack of moustache or beard. There are also four swan-like birds and the woman is holding two of them by the neck, one in either hand.

1–4 The celebrated walrus-ivory box known as the 'Franks Casket' (all except one side in the British Museum). Carved in seventh-century Northumbria, the casket is remarkable for its mixture of scenes drawn from the Bible, classical and Anglo-Saxon myth and history. The variety of these scenes presupposes a cultured man (whether the artist or designer) who was at home not only in his own pagan Anglo-Saxon traditions but also in the learning of Greece and Rome. He was no more inconsistent than a modern practising Christian in accepting equally the myth and the historical event. *Opposite:* The panel *above* (original now in the Bargello, Florence), pictures incidents from the Old Scandinavian epic of Sigurd (Siegfried); the *centre* panel has Romulus and Remus suckled by the wolf; the back panel *below* depicts the siege of Jerusalem by the Roman Emperor Titus in AD 70.

The situation is this: that if we had no other means of reconstructing the Wayland story apart from our English remains it is a million to one that despite the clues scattered about in *Beowulf, Deor's Lament, Waldere* and the panel of the Franks Casket we should ever have hit on the correct solution. That we *are* able to solve the problem is due to Norse writings and particularly to the *Lay of Volund* (i.e. Wayland), found in the collection of ancient poems known as the *Verse Edda*. The unravelling of the threads of his myth forms a most instructive exercise which admonishes us that with outside help we may often clothe with flesh the bones of other Waylands lying embedded in our native sources. I can hardly stress this argument too much, for it has been, and still is, the fashion to urge the utmost caution in the use of ancient Scandinavian material for throwing light on the mythological and religious beliefs of our Anglo-Saxon forebears. We have been too careful: for over-cautious scholars would have us sacrifice too much. Think, for instance, how they would have denied us the story I am about to relate of Wayland if the pieces of the Franks Casket had really been thrown out of the French farmhouse into the midden and had never survived the covetous ignorance of youth or the unscrupulousness of dealers to find its way after over a thousand years to the British Museum; or if the crackling fragment of the Old English epic *Waldere* had never been rescued (as by pure chance it was) from a dilapidated bookbinding in Copenhagen in 1860; or if the unique *Beowulf* manuscript instead of being merely scorched had perished in the fire at Ashburnham House in 1731. All we should have been left with would have been the reference to Wayland in *Deor's Lament*: hardly enough to persuade the cautious that Anglo-Saxon *Weland* and Norse *Völundr* were really one and the same person in spite of a gap of five hundred years or so between the English and Norse writing down of their tale.

The three main characters in the Wayland story are Wayland himself, King Nidhad and his daughter Beadohild. These three occur in the Norse version as Volund, Nidud and Bodvild, and these are the forms I shall use while recounting this Norse version of their tale.

Three swan-maidens flew from the south over Murkwood to Wolf-dales 'to fulfil their fate'. They alighted by the shore of a lake where they occupied their time in spinning precious flax. Their names were Allwise, Swanwhite and Olrun and they were all princesses.

Three brothers, Egil, Slagfid and Volund, sons of the King of the Finns, found these maidens by the shore and Egil took Olrun, Slagfid took Swanwhite while Allwise threw her arms 'round the white neck of Volund'. Seven years they lived in love; during the eighth the maidens were disturbed with longing to return to Murkwood; and in the ninth year they fled. The three princes came home from hunting to find their lovers departed: Egil went east searching for Olrun, Slagfid went west for Swanwhite, but Volund waited alone in Wolfdales. There he worked at his craft of jeweller and metalsmith.

Nidud lord of the Niars was told of Volund's being alone in Wolf-dales and in the night he sent armed men whose corselets and shields

38

40

5 Franks Casket front panel, a mixture of Anglo-Saxon myth and Christian story.
On the left, in a composite picture, the lamed Wayland working at his anvil holds
the head of one of King Nidhad's sons in his tongs, another figure is connected
either with Wayland's flight or with the Swan maidens. On the right, the Magi
(named in runes) bring their gifts to the infant Jesus held in his mother's arms in the
stable with the star overhead.

glinted in the light of the waning moon. Volund was away on snowshoes,
hunting. The riders stole one of Volund's cunningly made rings.

When the hunter returned he fed his fire with brushwood and fir
branches to roast his bear's flesh, then he sat on a bearskin rug and counted
his rings. He saw that one was missing and believed his lover Allwise
had returned to him. He sat so long that he fell asleep only to be wakened
when he felt his wrists pinioned and his legs fettered.

He was dragged before King Nidud who accused him of stealing his
gold. Nidud kept for himself Volund's sword but the ring he gave to his
daughter Bodvild. Nidud's queen said, 'He shows his teeth when he
sees the sword and recognizes the ring on Bodvild's finger. His glittering
eyes are threatening as a serpent's: let his leg sinews be cut and set him
down on the island of Sævarstod.'

So Volund was hamstrung and marooned on a small island near the
shore of the mainland and there set to forge and fashion all kinds of
jewellery work. No one bar the King was allowed to visit him. Always
he hankered after his cunningly tempered blade now slung from Nidud's
belt and yearned for his lover's golden ring now adorning Bodvild's
finger: he never slept but plied his hammer and planned revenge.

Nidud's two young sons made their way slyly to the island of Sævarstod and Volund's smithy. They demanded the keys of his chest and to
see all his treasures, jewels and gems. Volund promised them that if they
told no one of their visit and came to see him next day, he would give
them all that treasure. When they returned he cut off their heads and hid

5

their bodies under the dungheap outside the smithy. He mounted their skulls in silver beneath the hair to make a present for Nidud their father; and from their eyes he worked precious stones which he sent to their mother; but of their teeth he craftily carved two breast ornaments for Bodvild. Bodvild was intrigued and curious to see the smith; she broke her ring stolen from Volund, making this an excuse secretly to visit him for she said, 'I dare tell no one save you alone.' Volund promised to repair the ring so that her father and mother would never know it had been broken. He gave her beer to drink and as she fell drowsy he violated her.

Then Volund cried that his wrongs were avenged and he rose in the air on wings he had contrived. But Nidud was left impotently to mourn his daughter's defilement and the death of his sons. . . .

What this story meant for the Old English it is not my intention to inquire. For them Wayland was the supreme craftsman, and these men of the period we have been pleased to call the 'Dark Ages' revered him for his workmanship and emulated him, as we are coming to realize more and more by what the spade turns up. Think only of the exquisite artistry of the treasures of Sutton Hoo. For us, their descendants, it is enough to note the similarity between Wayland and the lame Greek god Hephaistos and to Daedalus who also soared on wings.

The really important conclusion for us to reach after studying Wayland Smith is that chance has played an extraordinary part in the survival of the written and graphic evidence of him: three of the native sources came within a hair's breadth of utter destruction and the fourth is so allusive as to be useless for reconstructing the original tale without outside help. What is true of Wayland is likely to be true of others. We may note, too, the remarkable agreement between Old English and Old Norse versions of the tale in spite of a difference of some four or five hundred years in the setting down of the story in England and Iceland. 'Wayland's Bones' are everywhere scattered about the Old English landscape; it will be my task to assemble as many as may be into an articulate skeleton and then to clothe that skeleton with flesh. Many bones are no doubt destroyed or lost for ever, and the resurrected being will have to limp, even as Wayland himself did of old.

Chapter Two
WHO WERE THE ENGLISH?

At first glance, the modern English appear to be a mongrel lot: Tennyson partly hit it off when he sang 'Saxon and Norman and Dane are we', but even so he was quite forgetting the ancient Britons. In addition, we must understand him to have meant by *Saxon* 'Angles, Saxons and Jutes'; by *Dane* 'Norwegians, Swedes and Danes' and by *Norman* 'Norwegians, Swedes, Danes and Celts'.

The ancient Britons who inhabited these islands at the time of Christ were themselves a mixture of tribes. The Romans who conquered the Britons during the first century A D and who later interbred with them, were a *mélange* of peoples from Gaul and Italy with (no doubt) a sprinkling of barbarian mercenaries from the north of Europe as well as more exotic elements from the East. As I say, a people bred from Briton crossed Saxon (after A D 450), crossed Dane (after A D 800), crossed Norman (after 1066) could well appear to be mongrel.

But none of these interbreedings was what might be called in genetical terms 'a violent out-cross' such as would have been the case if Britain had been successfully invaded by an armada of Chinese or Red Indians or African Bushmen. Apart from any alteration in physical appearance that would have befallen the new Island Race under such circumstances, one has only to suppose a pagoda in Canterbury, a totem-pole in Trafalgar Square and rock-paintings on the Cheddar Gorge to begin to imagine the cultural changes which would have ensued.

Even the ancient Britons were comparatively near relations of the Angles, Saxons and Jutes, while the Danes and Normans were first cousins: and so the mongrelism of the English turns out to be more apparent than real.

The story of who the modern English originally were can be conveniently divided into three parts, the first dealing with the primitive stocks who were their ancestors of some six thousand years ago; the second dealing with the group of peoples whom we find in North-West Europe at the birth of Christ; and third, the allied tribes who after A D 450 crossed from Europe to England to form the English nation.

All the different tribes who go to make up the English were descendants of peoples whom it used to be the fashion to call Aryans but who

6

are now usually referred to as Indo-Europeans. One ought to recognize at the start that the term 'Indo-European' is not a racial but a linguistic one. It is beyond dispute that some six thousand years ago there roamed about eastern Europe or western Asia a group of peoples linked together by a language sufficiently of a piece to be called original Indo-European. Yet no archaeologist digging in the ground has ever pierced the skull or run his pick between the ribs of a skeleton of an original Indo-European. Nor will any digger ever do so. In spite of which, there is no doubt that (apart from Finnish, Basque, Magyar and Etruscan) the languages of Europe and many of India have developed from this distinct tongue which we call Indo-European.

The date at which this language was spoken can only be guessed at; and according to Professor P. S. Noble we have to go back to 4000 B C to find Indo-European still a linguistic unity. No one can say for certain whether the speakers of this Indo-European first came from Europe or Asia. The argument for and against is still going on. Clues from the vocabulary of the parent language suggest that original Indo-European speakers had reached a level of culture of the Later Stone Age. To this day in the languages of their descendants there are words of a common origin which indicate that the speakers of the parent tongue used weapons and tools made of stone. For instance, the Lithuanian *akmuo* meaning 'stone' and the Greek *akmon* meaning 'anvil' come from the same original, as do Old Norse *hamarr* 'hammer' and modern English 'hammer'; while Anglo-Saxon *seax* 'dagger' came from the same Indo-European word as Latin *saxa* meaning 'rock'.

It is rewarding to speculate from what we know of Indo-European vocabulary as to the kind of life its speakers led. We can say they were hunters and graziers wandering after wild beasts and fresh pasture; but they also knew how to sit down in one place, for a season at least, to enable them to plough, cultivate, sow and harvest a crop. They were able to grind grain and bake it into bread. Their vocabulary tells us that Indo-European speakers knew the ox, cow, horse, sheep and pig as well as the goose and duck, but they did not know the ass, camel, lion, tiger nor elephant. Whatever else they drank, they certainly recognized the uses of milk. It is important to understand something of their family life: the words for father, mother, brother, sister, son, daughter and grandchild are all original Indo-European. 'Widow' is original and so is 'daughter-in-law' but not 'son-in-law'. One may deduce from this that among Indo-Europeans it was customary for the son when he married to take his wife to live in his father's house; while married daughters went to live with their husband's parents. This communal family system is still in vogue today among some nations of Indo-European connection. We know little more about their tribal government than that they had chiefs and were accustomed to thrash out problems affecting the group in a sort of committee meeting of the elders.

We have no inscriptions or manuscripts in original Indo-European, but the mother-tongue can be roughly reconstructed since we know that although languages constantly change so that one never speaks

6 The invading Anglo-Saxons probably rowed across to Britain in open boats
similar to this one cut into a rock from Häggeby, Upland, Sweden *c.* AD 500.

today the tongue one spoke yesterday, nevertheless the changes are of a
regular order. Changes in the sound of words follow certain 'phonetic
laws'. One of the first great sound changes split the Indo-European dia-
lects into two groups: on one side stand Baltic, Slavonic, Indic, Iranian,
and Armenian, on the other Celtic, Greek, Albanian, Tocharian and the
language spoken by the forefathers of the present-day Germans, Frisians,
Dutch, Scandinavians, Icelanders and English. The test word in Indo-
European which serves to divide the sheep from the goats is the name
for the numeral 100. In Baltic, Slavonic, Indic, Iranian and Armenian
the primitive palatal *k* sound was changed into a sibilant *s* and therefore
these languages are known from their pronunciation of this old word for
100 as the *satem* tongues; the rest converted palatal *k* into ordinary *k* and
are therefore called the *kentum* tongues. By a later sound change affecting
only the primitive North West European tribes the consonant *k* became
h under certain conditions and so the Germans say 'hundert', the Dutch
'honderd', the Icelanders 'honðrað', ourselves 'hundred' while the
Romans for instance said 'centum' with a hard *c*.

There is nothing unique in such a sound change as split the early
tongues into *satem* and *kentum* groups, there is nothing geographically
significant about it with *satem* peoples in the east and *kentum* peoples in
the west as was at first supposed. Recent discoveries have brought to
light a *kentum* people in Asia Minor (the Hittites) and another as far east
as China (the Tocharian speakers). But the division into *satem* and *kentum* peoples does help to date the occasions when the Indo-European

speakers began to separate. It has been suggested already that Indo-European was a linguistic unity round about 4000 B C. It is fairly certain that by 2500 B C the Indo-European peoples had begun to drift apart, some to the ends of Europe, some to Asia Minor, some to India and some even as far as China. It seems that Indo-European had split into *satem* and *kentum* groups by 1500 B C and we know that a *kentum*-speaking people, the Italici, were present in Upper Italy by this time; while a *satem*-speaking people step from the thicker mists of prehistory about 1400 B C when we find them as rulers of a non-Indo-European-speaking race round about the Upper Euphrates River.

It is not necessary for my purpose to follow the individual tribes to their destinations: it is enough to have drawn attention to the strong cultural affinities of peoples like the Hindus, Greeks, Romans, Celts and the northern tribes from whom the English sprang. That there are communities in Europe whose language places them quite apart is, of course, everyday knowledge. As I have said, the Basques are such a people, the Hungarians and Finns are others. Even so, the languages of these 'strangers' often help to throw light on the beliefs of our own ancestors, especially when words have been borrowed by one from the other. Such a word is the Finnish *taivas* which was loaned from Indo-European and which, as we shall see when we ask who god was, points like a revealing finger at the sky.

It is important, if we are to understand our own mythology, to explore the relationship existing between the northern peoples, that branch of the Indo-European speakers who were the ancestors of the present-day Germans, Frisians, Dutch, Danes, Swedes, Norwegians, Icelanders and English. This group has been called in the past the Germanic or Teutonic nations: both names are ambiguous, for a part has come to be used for the whole, while both terms have an undesirable emotional colouring. I therefore propose to use a phrase formed in the same way as 'Indo-European' and to call the ancestors of the Germans, Frisians, Dutch, Danes, Swedes, Norwegians, Icelanders and English after the part of the Continent we first find them inhabiting in historical times the 'North West Europeans'.

I have already mentioned the disagreement as to where the Indo-European-speaking peoples originated – whether in Europe or in Asia; there can be no disagreement if, in dealing with the North West Europeans, we go no further back in time than when they were already settled in Europe. All their own native traditions on the subject point to a home in the north, to the southern tip of the Scandinavian Peninsula. Our early English literature remembers dimly this ancient seat when, for instance, the seventh-century Anglo-Saxon epic poem *Beowulf* refers to a culture hero called in the poem Scyld Scefing. Although *Beowulf* implies that the hero's main name was Scyld or 'Shield' after whom the ancient Danes were called Scyldings, it is certain that his real appellation was Sceaf or 'Sheaf'. The *Anglo-Saxon Chronicle* says Sceaf was born in Noah's Ark, *se wæs geboren on þære earce Noés*, an obvious Christianizing of a pagan legend – one of the first, but by no means the last we are likely to come across: the original pagan tale says Sceaf floated as a child from the sea in an open boat which stranded on the shores of Scania. According to the Old English chronicler Ethelwerd who died about the year 1000:

> Sceaf, in an open boat, was driven ashore on an island of Ocean called Scani. Weapons were piled up around him. He was only a baby and quite unknown to the inhabitants of those parts; nevertheless, they took him in and brought him up carefully as one of the family, afterwards electing him their king.

Another version by William of Malmesbury who died about 1142 runs as follows:

> Sceaf as a boy was wafted in a boat without oars to a certain island of Germany, Scandza (the same of which Jordanes speaks). He was sleeping, his head pillowed on a sheaf of corn: that is why he was called Sceaf and looked on as a living miracle by the folk of thereabouts and carefully brought up. When he became a man he ruled in the town called Slaswic, now Haithebi. That district is called Old Anglia being situated between the Saxons and the Goths. From this area the Angles came to Britain.

The historian of the Goths called Jordanes, to whom Malmesbury refers, was writing in the sixth century: he was confirmed in his belief that tribe after tribe flitted out of Scandinavia. Jordanes, in his *On the Goths* (Chapter 4), coined two phrases for Scandinavia to express his view, namely *officina gentium* 'a factory of peoples' and *vagina nationum* 'a womb of nations' (*Ex hac igitur Scandza insula quasi officina gentium aut certe velut vagina nationum . . . quondam memorantur egress*). Forms of the name Scandza used by Jordanes crop up in new settlements made by the migrating North West European tribes who nostalgically incorporated the name abroad just as their descendants did hundreds of years later when they colonized the New World and called their settlements New Amsterdam, New Jersey, New Orleans or New York: for example, after leaving southern Sweden the Goths founded Gothiscandza, the Langobards referred to their new home as Scatenauga, while the wandering Burgundians changed their name to Scandauii.

Traditions of an original northern home of the North West European peoples which at present answers to Scania, but which it seems at first included the Danish islands and possibly Denmark itself, are supported by place- and river-names. The archaic Scandinavian tribal names belong to the Bronze Age and have clearly come into being on the spot: as Firdir from 'fiords', Skeynir from Skaun 'the fair districts', Fervir from Fjære 'the ebb shore'.

History confirms a northern starting-point for the wanderings of the North West Europeans and a continuous southern march after about 200 BC. From then right up to the eleventh-century expeditions of the later Viking Age the movement of peoples has been a definite fanning out from north to south: North West Europeans trudged and tramped, boated and rode over the whole of northern Europe, through France

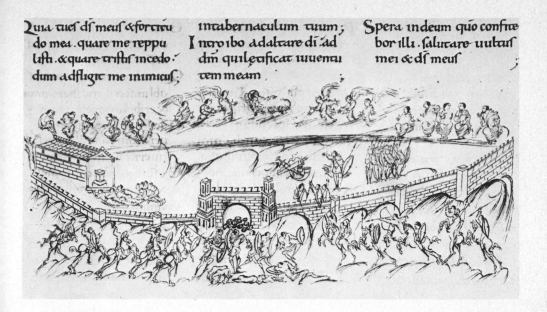

7–9 The massive walls of Burgh Castle Saxon Shore fort in Suffolk ('the work of giants') still stand to an impressive height with bastions at regular intervals. Already lying abandoned in the fields, such forts must have been the inspiration for the illustrator of the ninth-century Utrecht Psalter (*above*).

and Spain to the coast of North Africa, to northern Italy, through eastern Europe to Russia and the shores of the Black Sea: and of course, to the British Isles.

It has long been recognized as a fallacy that 'God made the country and man made the town.' As far as the English landscape is concerned one might claim with justice that it is almost entirely man-made, and the two tools which have wrought most change are the axe and the plough. Our English ancestors were both active woodcutters and persistent ploughmen. They came to a 'land all covered with trees' (the forest of the Weald, for instance, was 120 miles long and 30 miles broad), and they at once began to chop and clear; they went on to break the heavier virgin soils of the lowland valleys with their heavy plough. Large tracts of the country were marshland: such were the Fens, Romney Marsh and a long stretch of Somerset from the Mendips nearly as far as Taunton. A cat's cradle of Roman roads spanned the land from shore to shore, running straight and angular up hill, down dale between city and city and military post and military post. But even before the end of the fourth century many of the stone-built cities were decaying; after the Saxon invaders came they lay empty to the winds and rain, peopled by frogs and bats. Some, like Silchester and Viroconium, were never lived in again, others such as Cambridge were derelict in Bede's time, while Chester was called a 'ghost town' by the chronicler of King Alfred's days. The English had always been countrymen; they did not take naturally to town life, preferring, instead of barracks of stone, the isolated farm or hamlet built of timber or lath and plaster. The ruins of Roman civilization in Britain appeared to our ancestors as a thing
7–9   divorced from the workaday world. The great forts, ramparts and paved roads were, in their estimation, hardly intended for human use but were (they said) 'the work of giants'. One anonymous poet describ-
27   ing in all probability the ruins of Roman Bath says:

> This stone, these walls are a matter for wonder. Broken by fate, the towers have tumbled down and the handiwork of giants drops to dust . . . but in times past many a light-hearted fellow sparkling with gold and jewels, proud and happy in his cups here preened himself in shining armour: there was treasure for him to see, silver, precious stones, riches, possessions, costly gems, and this bright citadel of a broad kingdom. . . .

The Saxons had been nibbling at Britain for two or three hundred years before the generally accepted date of their removing here, AD 450. In fact, a band of Saxon raiders seems to have thrust its way far up country in 429. It is curious too (to say the least) that many of the early leaders of the English invasions have British names, Cerdic and Ceawlin for example, a fact which suggests that intermarriage between Britons and Saxons had been taking place for some time. For what more natural than that British wives should choose the names of their offspring by Saxon fathers and, moreover, should call the boys after their British uncles and grandfathers? It is obvious that from the middle of the third century onwards the Romano-Britons became increasingly uneasy: it is not difficult to imagine with what uneasiness owners of villas overlooking the Channel and North Sea must have scanned the grey horizon for hostile craft. The imperial authorities were worried enough to plan a reorganization of the defences of Britain as we can tell from the *Notitia Dignitatum*. This is an official nominal roll of the military and civil dignitaries of both the Eastern and Western Roman Empires, together with names of places at which they were stationed and the number of troops under their command. The garrison which had to defend Britain against the Angles, Saxons and Jutes was disposed as follows.

There was a Northern Command under the Duke of the (five) Britains (*Dux Britanniarum*). The Duke had his headquarters at York, where as of old there was based the Sixth Legion 'Victrix', and a number of auxiliary troops. There was a Coastal Command under the Count of the Saxon Shore (*Comes Litoris Saxonici*) with headquarters at Richborough in Kent where the Second Legion, 'Augusta', had been wholly or partly drafted from the borders of Wales. The Count of the Saxon Shore's forts were massive and extensive varying from six to ten acres in area, with ditches and bastions and walls in places rising to twenty-five feet. They were each equipped with an establishment of 500 or 1000 men; and they stretched at intervals from Brancaster in Norfolk to Porchester in Hampshire. But in face of the oncoming flood they were like a dam built of isolated pebbles intended hopefully to hold back an ocean: and like eroded pebbles their remains are visible to this day.

This is no place for me to attempt to throw a great light on that darkest age of Britain round about AD 400 when through internal collapse, through usurpation or defection of Roman generals, or through invitation of local British rulers, or because wide tracts of the country lay wasted by pillage and open for the taking, the Angles, Saxons and Jutes were enabled to change their tip-and-run tactics, their raids-in-force into a permanent occupation of the British Isles. It is perhaps enough to say that the Saxons coasted from Holstein and as far south as the rivers Ems, Rhine, Sieg and Unstrut; that the Angles moved from the district still called Angeln between Schleswig and Flensburg; while the Jutes rowed off from the banks of the Lower Rhine. There can be little doubt that the Angles, Saxons and Jutes were a mixture of many tribal elements: though after they had been settled a few generations in England, Angles were being addressed as Saxons, Saxons were calling themselves Angles and the whole conglomeration was being referred to as Englishmen and their language as English speech.

The opinion of modern historians appears to be that the Anglo-Saxon occupation of Britain was certainly not achieved by a series of set campaigns, with lines of communication, bridgeheads, consolidations and advances, but was on the whole a sort of muscling-in. The towns of Roman Britain were decaying anyway; the villas had done the same because they had lost their slaves, but some villages may have been another matter. According to T. C. Lethbridge in *Merlin's Island* villages seem to have lived on with a hybrid population:

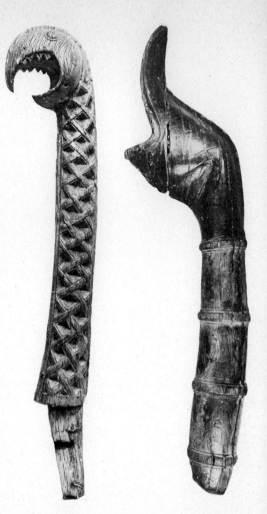

10, 11 Two Viking ships' figure-heads
found in the River Scheldt; both portray
fearsome monsters, frequently met with
in myth and epic, *left* a dragon, *right* a
serpent. At sea, the figure-head frightened
off evil sprites; in harbour, the dragon or
serpent could be removed so as not to
scare the *Landvettir*, the good spirits of the
countryside.

> The fact is that, although we call these people Anglo-Saxons, we can be by
> no means certain that they did not almost instantly become a hybrid race. . . .
> In most cases I believe that the immigrants married a high percentage of
> British women and that, in a generation or two their whole material culture
> had altered as a result of it.

This appears to be an extreme view, and against it there is the orthodox
opinion expressed by Miss Dorothy Whitelock, namely that:

> . . . there is, in fact, little indication that the invaders' civilisation was affected
> to any appreciable extent by the outlook and institutions of the pre-English
> inhabitants.

This conclusion is supported by such facts as the extraordinarily small
influence exerted by the language of the natives on that of the new-
comers; that the Anglo-Saxon word for a Briton came to mean 'slave';
and that the upland British villages were deserted for the valleys which
37   the English cleared with the axe and worked with their heavy plough.

12 Thumb-ring from the Snape ship-burial; gold, set with a Roman intaglio, this is the finest jewel ever found in such burials before the uncovering of the Sutton Hoo boat.

13 Wayland's Smithy, a name given to a Neolithic long barrow by the Anglo-Saxons. Situated on the Ridgeway, not far from the White Horse of Uffington, the huge stones of the barrow could only have been set there by gods or giants – according to our invading ancestors.

14, 15 The Gokstad ship rising from its grave
at Vestfed on Oslo Fiord in 1880. King Olaf
Geirstada-Alf was buried in this vessel, a
Viking who, according to the old Icelandic
writer Snorri Sturluson, was 'strikingly
handsome, very strong and large of growth',
but crippled with arthritis as shown by his
skeleton. When restored (*right*) the Gokstad
ship was used as a model for a full-sized replica
which successfully sailed the Atlantic in 1893,
from Bergen to Chicago.

16 The importance of the ship in death as in life for our ancestors is shown in cemeteries where graves are shaped like boats, as in this one from Vätteryd, Scania, Sweden. On to these shores, in the far-distant past, was cast an open boat with a living baby lying on a sheaf of corn. Rescued and brought up by the countryfolk, Scyld Scefing became their king and when he died (according to *Beowulf*) his people gave him a Viking's funeral, setting him adrift in a splendid vessel, his corpse piled round with arms and heirlooms: 'no one, no counsellor in the hall. could tell for certain, ever, who received that burden' (p. 91).

17, 18 A clinker-built, iron-nailed ship having neither mast nor sail found at Nydam, Denmark. Propelled by oars, the Nydam boat is essentially similar to the one dug up at Sutton Hoo (Ill. 47) and of the type in which the Anglo-Saxons rowed to Britain. The Oseberg ship (*opposite*) from Oslo shows in its graceful lines, its sophisticated steering oar, mast and sail some four hundred years of shipbuilding development.

It is quite certain that the Old English still looked towards the Continent and did so for many generations. Their earliest songs and epics deal with a European scene and with heroes like Beowulf, Hrothgar, Waldere, Finn, Hnæf and many others whose homes and exploits were in Denmark, Sweden and even farther east. The consciousness of their origin from and their strong links with the North West Europeans continued long in the new land. In fact, even before all England was converted to Christianity the English were sending missionaries to Germany to convert their relatives; for, as the English monk St Boniface wrote home in 783, 'Have pity on them, because even they themselves are accustomed to say, "We are of one blood and one bone."'

Both the English and German appreciation of such tenacious links (still strong some three hundred years after the Anglo-Saxon invasion) reminds us that ideas are almost indestructible, that folk-memory is tough and the mind of man in general prefers the security of tradition to the uncertainty of what is new. When men move it is usually because they are being pushed. Whatever it was that pushed our forefathers from the Continent, this is hardly the place to inquire. They reached Britain *14, 15, 17,* in open boats loaded to the gunwales with their household belongings, *18, 19* their pots and bowls and little wooden buckets bound with bronze. Pigs and sheep no doubt lay hog-tied under the thwarts to prevent their leaping into the waves: poultry, heaps of protesting feathers, were *20* in a similar case. Here and there a horse would stick its surprised head and swivelling ears over the side: the shouts of the rowers would mingle with the lowing of cattle. For the Angles, Saxons and Jutes were farmers

19 Stave-built bucket from Sutton Hoo. The Anglo-Saxons brought such household gear in their open boats to Britain. This one was buried in a ship presumably for its occupant's use at the end of his voyage to the after-life.

20 Detail from the Bayeux Tapestry stitched in England after the Norman Conquest showing Viking-type ships with figure-heads carrying men and horses (*see also* Ill. 10).

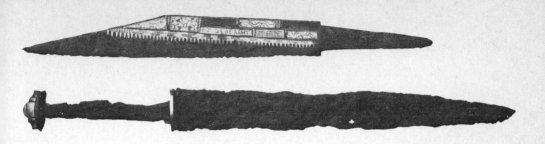

21 Typical Anglo-Saxon weapons. A scramaseax, or single-bladed knife, from Sittingbourne, Kent, engraved with the name GEBEREHT, and a long sword from a seventh-century grave in Winchester.

22 Viking spear-head inlaid with silver and bronze found in the River Thames.

in a small way of business and their livestock had to be lugged along as surely as their ploughs and harrows. They tended to congregate in hamlets made up of clutters of tiny huts with floors sunk a couple of feet below ground-level. They appear, these first settlers, to have lived in squalor: excavations by Lethbridge at Waterbeach and West Row have uncovered a litter of bones on the hut floors together with potsherds, ashes and the occasional dead dog. Of course, there were buildings of a grander nature such as the fine hall called Heorot described in *Beowulf*: these were the abodes of the aristocracy, and it is only a matter of recent years since the first ever of these has been dug up. In 1956 an Anglo-Saxon site at Yeavering, Northumberland on being excavated revealed a township with four halls each nearly a hundred feet long, two of them having a porch at both ends. Another building appears to have been a pagan temple.

    The everyday garments of the Angles, Saxons and Jutes were cut by the housewife from coarse homespun cloth, though for party wear they possessed finer and more complicated textiles. The men may have worn cross-gartered loose trousers and a kind of tunic, though no material remains have been found. Sometimes they went barelegged, for bangles

24

23

23 Reconstruction of the royal halls at Yeavering whose site was discovered in 1956. Remains of post holes provide essential evidence for the re-creation of the main buildings. Yeavering was burned down probably by Cadwalla.

24 A typical Anglo-Saxon house built over a sunken pit reconstructed from finds at Bourton-on-the-Water. Similar houses have been excavated at Sutton Courtenay, Berkshire and at Linford, Essex. A number of houses, including this one, have produced evidence for upright looms and clay loom weights.

25 Burning Romano-British villas left behind by Saxon settlers on their march across Britain.

have been discovered on their dug-up ankle bones. There are no hob-nails from heavy boots such as are common in Romano-British graves: our ancestors were accustomed to treading earth and grass tracks, not paved ways. All grown men carried home-made weapons, normally a rather rough six-foot spear, an angular sheath-knife stuck in a belt, and *21, 22* less frequently a long straightsided iron sword. The sword, almost always a flat simple two-edged blade about thirty inches long and two and a half broad, was owned (judging from finds), by only one man in twenty. Remains of circular wooden shields, about two feet in diameter with ridged iron bosses in the middle to protect the grasping fist, are numerous. The womenfolk frequently adorned themselves with two and sometimes three brooches, often with festoons of glass and amber *34, 35* beads looped from brooch to brooch. Their waists were spanned by a girdle from which might hang characteristic T-shaped iron or bronze *26* trinkets, ivory rings, strike-a-lights and knives.

And together with their worldly goods, the Angles, Saxons and Jutes brought along the furnishings of their minds. As to the mytho-logical furniture, before most of it was re-upholstered or thrown out by zealous missionaries and their even more ardent converts, I now hope to inquire.

26 Women's bronze girdle-hooks with characteristic T-shape from Soham,
Cambridgeshire.

Chapter Three

OLD ENGLISH HEATHENISM

Because of what (at first sight) appears to be the scarcity of heathen remains in England, some scholars have asked themselves the question, were the Old English really heathen? And in the last fifty years there has been a tendency to answer with a 'well, not really'. Such historians as Oman and Hodgkin seem to have come to the conclusion that our ancestors of fifteen hundred years ago were hardly paying more than lip-service to heathenism and that (as Hodgkin puts it) their pagan faith did not stand the sea-crossing from the Continent at all well.

This is a point of view and it is not easy from the available evidence to rebut it: for the known facts are that the Angles, Saxons and Jutes rowed over from Europe to Britain about A D 450, settled and farmed England fairly rapidly, received the first Christian missionaries led by the Italian monk Augustine in A D 597, and were more or less converted to a Christian people by A D 664 the date of the Synod of Whitby. That is to say, within a couple of lifetimes of the traditional settlement by Hengist and Horsa in Thanet Christian preachers had landed at the same spot, and within another Biblical life span the English had been converted. It would have been possible for most Englishmen who were Christians in the year of the Synod of Whitby to say 'My grandfather was a heathen' just as their descendants of today who are agnostics, atheists, subscribers to curious cults or mere nondescripts can say 'My grandfather was a Christian.'

The difficulty of deciding how far the Angles, Saxons and Jutes were practising heathens is mainly of the Church's making: usually, no opponents fight more bitterly and to the death than warring religions. True, the winner will sometimes wear its opponent's creeds like scalps – but not round the waist: every effort is made to obliterate the memory of whence the creed came and the scalp is worn like a toupee and passed off as real hair. The Christian religion had done this in the very beginning when it was struggling for dear life against the Hellenistic faiths of the eastern Mediterranean and Christ was duelling with Attis and Adonis and Osiris and especially Mithras; Christianity adopted alien ideas again when in England the missionary monks acted on the advice of Pope Gregory the Great and incorporated local heathen customs into the

28 (*opposite*) Nine Romano-British forts under the command of the Count of the Saxon Shore. Sited to repel barbarian invaders, they covered the coastline from the Wash to Porchester. In this fifteenth-century copy of a page from the fifth-century *Notitia Dignitatum* the forts named in Latin are Bradwell, Dover, Lympne, Brancaster, Burgh (Ills. 7–9), Reculver, Richborough, Pevensey and Porchester.

27 Roman Bath, the type of ruins which filled the country-loving Anglo-Saxons with awe akin to fear.

.F L.
INTAIL.
COMORD.
.PR.

othona. Dubris.

Lemannis. Branoduno. Garianno.

Regulbi. Rutupis. Anderidos.

Portuadurm.

29 Christianity assimilates elements of ancient Greek religion: a third-century A D mosaic of Christ-Helios in the necropolis below St Peter's, Rome.

30 Wansdyke, the great ditch and rampart of Woden cutting across the English countryside from Hampshire to Somerset.

conduct of the Christian year. Once Christianity was accepted in England the Church had no compunction about obliterating the memory of the heathen origin while retaining the custom of Yule-tide and harvest festivals for instance, or of the charming (now *blessing*) of the plough. The obliteration of heathenism from written records (not so from the lips of men) was particularly easy. It was easy because reading and writing were a Church monopoly with the result that what heathen literary memories remain have done so largely due to oversight. It is not to be expected that the writers in the cool cell and shady cloister would lend their quills to propaganda of the heathen gods. And because we moderns subscribe to the belief (or pretend we do) that 'the pen is mightier than the sword', we are apt to discount evidence which is unwritten, except where such evidence is of itself conclusive or verifiable from written sources: one of our modern shibboleths is that we must have everything in writing. It is a good thing that our pagan ancestors have, so to speak, writ large their heathendom on the English landscape. The gods of the English still in place-names retain a firm hold on the countryside. It is into the news of the old mythology offered by Anglo-Saxon villages and towns that I now propose to inquire.

31 One of the god Woden's by-names was Grim. Up and down the country run a number of earthworks called by our ancestors Grim's Ditch or Dyke. This one is two and a half miles west of Downton, Wiltshire.

32 The Vale of Pewsey, an area associated with the worship of Woden, but having religious affinities going even further back into the Early Iron Age, as evidenced by the White Horse cut into the chalk of the hillside.

Place-names of Anglo-Saxon origin give us two kinds of information about the old religion: first, they call to mind the names of some of the gods and supernatural beings and secondly, they indicate former shrines or holy places. At least three gods and one goddess can be shown from place-names to have been venerated in Anglo-Saxon England. The gods are Woden, Thunor and Tiw, and the goddess, Frig. We gather from a study of place-names and other sources that Woden was chief god. Traces of his cult are scattered more widely over the rolling English countryside than those of any other heathen deity, and he is the only one we know of at present whose works were commemorated by a nick-name. We are sure that Woden was worshipped in Kent, Essex, Hampshire, Wiltshire, Somerset, Staffordshire, Bedfordshire and Derbyshire. An important centre of Woden's influence appears to have been above the Vale of Pewsey where the notable earthwork called Wansdyke   *32* (Wodnes dic) runs from Hampshire to Somerset. Near by are spots   *30* formerly known as *Wodnes beorh* 'Woden's barrow' now Adam's Grave in the bounds of Alton Priors, and *Wodnes denu* 'Woden's valley' in the bounds of West Overton. There was a similar centre at Wednesbury 'Woden's fortress' and Wednesfield 'Woden's plain' above the headwaters of the River Thame. Other place-names incorporating Woden are Woodnesborough (near Sandwich) and Wornshill (near Sittingbourne), nor does that exhaust the list. Some light on the chief god's attributes is thrown by places which enshrine one of his nicknames,

Grim. This word denotes a person wearing a hood in such a way as to mask the face and is related to the Old Norse Grimr, a name applied to Odinn on account of his habit of wandering between the worlds in disguise. Many earthworks in southern England are called Grimsdyke: they attest the awe in which Woden was held as the supposed creator of these vast ramparts, while at the same time suggesting the popular nature of his cult in that here a nickname is used. Woden was not only the ancestor of kings, he was also worshipped by the three principal races of which the English nation was composed, as we may gather from the appearance of his name in Jutish Kent, Saxon Essex and Wessex and in Anglian Mercia.

Thunor, god of thunder, was a friend of the common man in his day, and that meant of the farmer. His name occurs much more often than Woden's in Essex and Wessex where he seems to have been the most generally honoured of the gods; but he was worshipped in Jutish territory too as we can guess from the lost *Thunores hlæw* 'Thunor's mound' in Thanet and *Thunores lea* 'Thunor's clearing' near Southampton. Modern examples of places once sacred to Thunor are Thunderfield (Surrey), Thundridge (Hertfordshire) and six spots in Sussex, Essex, Surrey and Hampshire in which his name precedes *-leah* an Old English word meaning a 'wood' or 'woodland clearing'. This *-leah* we find joined also to Woden's and Tiw's names providing corroborative evidence of the Roman historian Tacitus' remarks associating the practical worship of the 'Germanic' gods with sacred groves.

The old god Tiw was remembered at Tuesley (Surrey) and the lost Tislea (Hampshire) and Tyesmere (Worcestershire); while the village-name Tysoe (Warwickshire) meaning 'Tiw's hill spur' clearly refers, says Sir Frank Stenton, 'to one of the projections which issue at this point from the escarpment above the Vale of the Red Horse. It is not improbable that the vale derived its name from the figure of a horse cut into the hillside as a symbol of Tiw. In any case, his association with one of the most commanding sites in the southern Midlands is an impressive testimony to the importance of his cult.'

Frig, mother of gods and men, is probably to be found in Freefolk (Hampshire) which has the form *Frigefolc* in Domesday Book and could mean 'Frig's people'. Two other places in the same county of Hampshire, Froyle and Frobury, seem to have caught and held Frig's name like a fly in amber to the puzzlement of later generations: Ekwall in his *Dictionary of English Place-names* says 'their names were once identical, apparently O.E. *Freohyll*, which may be "the hill of the goddess Frig".' Fryup in the North Riding of Yorkshire may be the *hop* or marshy enclosure of Freo, i.e. Frig. The goddess's name also crops up in the East Riding village of Frydaythorpe.

There are a number of place-names bearing witness to our ancestors' belief in supernatural beings other than gods, beings who in some cases were enemies of the gods. Grimly and Greenhill in Warwickshire take their first element from O.E. *grima* and mean in one case the wood, and in the other the hill haunted by a ghost or sprite. Similarly, a cliff visited

33 A diseased man molested by one of the bands of supernatural beings believed by our ancestors to surround them. In this case the victim is injured by elf-shot. (From the ninth-century Utrecht Psalter.)

by a spectre (O.E. *scinna*) is Shincliffe in County Durham; while Sho-brooke (Devon), Shuckburgh (Warwickshire) and Shucknall (Hereford) stand for the brook or hills whose visitant is a goblin (O.E. *scucca*). Interesting are Thirsford (Norfolk) and Tusmore (Oxfordshire) with a first element from O.E. *thyrs* and meaning respectively 'giant's ford' and 'giant's mere'. In his *History of the Anglo-Saxons* R.H. Hodgkin says of the Old English giants that they were 'not of the stuff to dream of waging war against the great gods', but he was really quite wrong. For it is evident from a couple of references in *Beowulf* (of which more later) that our forebears knew the story of how the giants had attacked the gods and how they had been repaid for their temerity by being over-whelmed in a universal flood. It is a story whose details are obscured by the mists of ages and the shadows of the cloister, but – as with Wayland – still called to mind by the Northmen. The 'witch's valley' is the meaning of Hascombe (Surrey) and Hescombe (Somerset) where the first element of the name is O.E. *hætse* or *hægtesse* 'witch'. Mythological animals are recalled in the lost *Nikerpoll* near Pershore (O.E. *nicor* 'water monster') and Drakelow in Derbyshire (O.E. *dracan hlaw* 'dragon's mound').

Three Old English words attest the strength of heathen worship in the land by the widespread frequency with which they occur: they are *ealh* a temple, *hearh* or *hearg* a hill-sanctuary, and *weoh* which means 'idol', 'shrine' or 'sacred spot'. *Ealh* is rarer than the others but may still be found in Alkham near Dover; it occurred too in Ealhfleot, an early name of a channel connecting Faversham with the sea. *Hearh* remains in Harrow-on-the-Hill (Middlesex), Harrowden (Bedford, Northants., Essex), Arrowfield Top (Worcs.) and Peper Harrow (Surrey). Com-monest of all and most widely distributed is *weoh* which lives on in Wye (Kent), Whiligh, Whyly, Willey (Surrey), Wheely Down, Weyhill (Hants), Weedon Beck, Weedon Lois (Northants.), Weedon (Bucks.), Weoley (Worcs.), Weeley (Essex), Wyville (Kesteven), Weeford (Staffs.), Wyham (Lincs.) and Patchway (Sussex).

From Old Icelandic literary sources we learn that the Northmen who were leaders of the time were able to combine the functions of temporal chief and heathen priest under the title of *godi*. It seems more than likely that the Anglo-Saxon observed the same custom by owning private

34 Jewels from the so-called Dark Ages, exquisite works of art in gold and silver and semi-precious stones. These pagan Anglo-Saxon ornaments include belt-plates from Mucking, a silver quoit-brooch from Sarre, a gold bracteate with three eagles and a long brooch and disc-brooch set with garnets, all from Dover.

shrines, for such must have been the lost *Cusanweoh* a seventh-century name of a place near Farnham in Surrey, the 'shrine of Cusa'; similarly there is in Sussex the already mentioned Patchway the 'shrine of Pæccel'. An extension of this private ownership to a group or family is presumably to be seen in the old name for Harrow-on-the-Hill which was *Gumeninga hearh* 'the sanctuary of the Gumenings' and the lost *Besingahearh* (Surrey) 'sanctuary of the Besings'.

The heathen cult-names are not evenly distributed over England: from the way in which they lie it is clear that the main strength of heathen feeling had rolled like a tide across Kent and the south-east up the centre of the country as far as the north Midlands. The most westerly of the known sites dedicated to the old gods is the lost *Thunresfeld* near Hardenhuish in Wiltshire; northwards, cult-names are rare between the Hum-

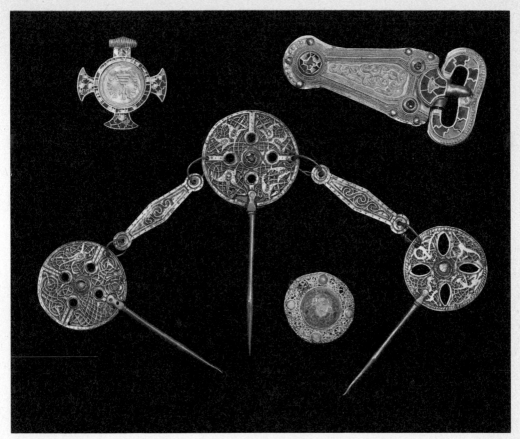

35 Anglo-Saxon jewellery showing Christian as well as pagan influences: a coin of the Byzantine Emperor Heraclius set in the form of a cross (Wilton); a buckle of gold filigree and garnets (Taplow); linked pins with animal decoration (Witham); and brooch of gold filigree and enamel (Dowgate Hill).

ber and Welland; and even more rare in Northumbria and East Anglia.

Such then, is the evidence of village, hill and field that the Old English had strong heathen beliefs; it is evidence more than enough to provide the answer 'yes' to Hodgkin's rhetorical question, 'Is it possible that the gods who appear so little in their place-names came much into their thoughts?'–a question which Hodgkin wished to answer 'no' – wrongly, as I believe.

But the further evidence to which I hope to call attention now and in later chapters, the literary evidence, has lately been suspect, particularly if it is not of native origin. Scholars have handled it as though it smelled. It will be my hope to remove some of the bad odour and some of the suspicion. Read, for instance, the words of Sir Frank Stenton (a brilliant historian of Anglo-Saxon England) who says:

In much that has been written about the subject [of Old English heathenism] in general, and about the gods of English heathenism in particular, scholars have drawn somewhat freely upon the abundant material which has survived from heathen Scandinavia. But the connexion between English and Scandinavian heathenism lies in a past which was already remote when the English peoples migrated to Britain. Much of the Scandinavian evidence has a sophisticated cast, and the danger of using it for the illustration of primitive English beliefs is steadily becoming clearer. It is equally dangerous to use the magical literature of the tenth and eleventh centuries as a line of approach towards the English pagan pre-world, for there is the strongest possibility that the Scandinavian influence has played upon the fragments of ancient literature which it incorporates.

Miss Dorothy Whitelock, brought up in the same tradition as Sir Frank Stenton, is also sympathetic to this view. She says:

It is often held that Anglo-Saxon poetry is permeated by a strong belief in the power of fate, inherited from heathen times, and some have even seen a conflict between a faith in an omnipotent Christian God and a trust in a blind, inexorable fate. To me this view seems exaggerated. . . . It would be natural enough that, even while yet heathen, the Anglo-Saxons should feel that man's destiny is outside his own control, stronger evidence would be necessary before we could assume a belief in the fate-weaving Norns at the foot of the world tree Yggdrasil, as described in the much later, poetic, mythology of the Scandinavians.

Perhaps this is the place to state my own views of the relationship between the full Scandinavian mythical sources and the broken English remains. It is clear that orthodox opinion regards the sources of Scandinavian mythology as likely to mislead if they are used to fill gaps in the picture of an Old English heaven, earth and hell peopled by gods, men and giants. Orthodoxy, it seems to me, has swung so far from what may be false that it is also away off the truth. Where both Old English and Old Norse parallel sources remain there is (with some exceptions to be discussed later) a large measure of agreement. I have already indicated one example, that of Wayland-Volund, a story where no connected account remains in Old English, but where other English sources show convincingly the complete correspondence of the Old English and Old Norse tales. I should now like to discuss another case of an Anglo-Saxon myth which orthodox opinion accepts without argument as being derived from the Old Testament but which can be demonstrated to be basically pagan and in fact of North West European and ultimately Indo-European provenance. I am referring to the myth of a World Flood.

References to the Flood are found in *Beowulf*. At line 111 the poet mentions supernatural creatures who (he says) were sprung from Cain, 'monsters, ettins and elves and orcs, also giants who battled against God for a long time; in the end he paid them out for it'. The way in which God paid out the giants is later described when the *Beowulf* poet speaks of an ancient sword-hilt which had the story cut on it in runes:

it had been written long ago: a tale of a struggle of former days in which a flood, a boiling ocean engulfed the race of giants. They had lived in pride, a people estranged from the eternal Lord, and for that the Ruler gave them their final requital in the whelming waters.

In his *History of the Anglo-Saxons* Hodgkin dismisses the story out of hand when he remarks that the Old English giants were not of the substance to fight the gods. The references just quoted from *Beowulf* give Hodgkin the lie.

On the other hand, Miss Dorothy Whitelock in the *Audience of Beowulf* (page 5) assumes without argument that the flood referred to in *Beowulf* is the Biblical Flood. On the face of it, we might be tempted to agree. After all, having experienced two thousand years of Christianity, it comes as a shock to us to be told that there are over five hundred different myths of a World Flood ranging from the Sumerian to Amerindian. Again, the beings in *Beowulf* who drown in the flood are said to be descended from Cain and they are punished by the Lord. But when we inquire into these apparently Biblical characters we find that they have nothing whatever to do with the Old Testament, and in fact, they are the 'ettins and elves and orcs, also giants' who have been lifted straight from the Anglo-Saxon pagan mythology. We then begin to suspect that the *Beowulf* poet was Christianizing pagan material – and so he was: such monsters as he names were part and parcel of the heathen mythology and had nothing to do with Cain until Old English converts tried to combine elements from their own pagan myth with the new Christian one. 'Ettins', 'elves' and 'orcs' are all words of native origin; 'giant' is not – it comes through the Latin from Greek. Because the *Beowulf* poet uses the word 'giant', which possibly came into English via the Vulgate Bible, Miss Whitelock assumes that he was lifting too the Biblical story of the Flood. Miss Whitelock goes on to say that the poet's audience must have understood the connection of the word 'giant' with the Vulgate because the poet offers no gloss for it. This argument is like Hodgkin's about the Old English giants not being of the stuff to fight against the gods – the text of *Beowulf* gives it the lie. For it is not until the poet has exhausted all the native words 'ettins and elves and orcs' that he adds a final synonym 'giants'.

The Bible story of the Flood tells how the *men* of the ancient world (not giants) were all drowned except one man, Noah and his dependants. The essential part of the myth is that Noah was saved in his Ark. The *Beowulf* myth tells of *giants* who fought against god and most significantly there is no mention of an Ark. It is unthinkable that a Christian poet writing of the Biblical Flood should have missed out the Ark.

Now, the heathen Scandinavian version of the Deluge says that three gods Odinn, Vili and Vé fell out with the race of giants and killed their leader Ymir whose blood poured forth to form the ocean in which all the other giants except Bergelmir and his wife were drowned. These two lived on to perpetuate the giant race. But the three gods created the earth out of Ymir's carcass, having created the sea from his blood.

36 A page of Anglo-Saxon charms against sickness and disease from the manuscript book *Lacnunga*.

This, I contend is much more likely to have been the version cut in runes on the sword described in *Beowulf*; and I have no doubt whatsoever that the poet was referring to an actual sword-hilt of ancient pagan workmanship which he himself had seen. Such an heirloom of our race stands in the same relationship to the Flood myth as the Franks Casket does to the Wayland Story: and who knows but what some day the spade may not turn it up?

It is admitted that later accounts of the Norse Deluge myth (after the sixteenth century) say that the giant Bergelmir escaped the flood by 'going up into his boat'. But a glance at the earliest manuscript dating to the thirteenth century shows that Bergelmir is said originally to have escaped by 'climbing up on to his mill' or mill-stand. This was not understood by later editors who substituted the word *bátr* (boat) for *lúðr* (mill or mill-stand), no doubt on the analogy of the Old Testament story.

As I have said, there are over five hundred World Flood myths deriving from both Eastern and Western Hemispheres. The Hebrew tale itself is a derivative of an earlier one, namely the ancient Mesopotamian story of Ut-Napishtim the Sumerian Noah. Its main situation is the saving of mankind. On the other hand, the Old English version as we have it in *Beowulf* is the same as the Norse one and ultimately related to the Greek version of the struggle between gods and giants. The North West European story is not a salvation myth at all – that at least is obvious – but is a creation myth giving one version of how the land, sea and air came into existence. As such it goes back to Indo-European times and takes its place as another of the hundreds of Flood myths still extant.

Such argument as the above is perhaps a little tedious: but it is necessary to scotch attempts at Christianizing pagan myths by modern writers as well as to reinforce my claim that more often than not the Old English and Old Norse versions of myth are in agreement, and that Norse sources are, in general, reliable guides to supplement our own.

But I myself shall argue that our Old English remains, both literary and other, hold far more evidence of the ancient heathenism than has yet been brought to light. It will be my purpose to show forth this evidence in the following pages: but before doing so, I would like to discuss some literary attestations of the heathen beliefs of our ancestors which are generally accepted by modern writers.

The Anglo-Saxon *Charms* bear witness to native pagan beliefs: these incantations are often difficult to interpret being a mixture of Old English, Latin, Greek, Celtic, Hebrew and Norse elements sometimes reduced to plain gibberish with a superficial Christianization to add to the confusion. The chief sources are two British Museum MSS. called *Leechbook* (Regius 12 D xvii) and *Lacnunga* (Harley 585) written between AD 950 and 1050. How truly ancient are the *Charms* may be gathered from a modern example for curing a sprain recorded in many parts of England, Scotland, Denmark, Norway, Sweden, Netherlands, Esthonia, Finland and Hungary:

36

> Our Lord rade
> his foal's foot slade;
> down he lighted,
> his foal's foot righted:
> bone to bone,
> sinew to sinew,
> blood to blood
> flesh to flesh
> heal in the name of the Father, Son and
>   Holy Ghost.

This *Charm* for a sprain is found a thousand years earlier in ninth-century Germany with the original pagan personages who were later to be superseded by 'Our Lord':

> Phol [i.e. Balder] and Woden
> rode to the wood

where Balder's foal
wrenched its foot . . .
then Woden charmed
as he well knew how:
as for bone-wrench
so for blood-wrench
so for limb-wrench;
'Bone to bone,
blood to blood,
limb to limbs,
as if they were glued.'

This *Second Merseburg Charm* as it is called can be paralleled by a similar one from the Hindu *Atharva-Veda* iv. 12 of about 500 BC, showing that 'Our Lord rade' is part of a body of material of Indo-European origin. In fact, the *Charms* reflect religious ideas which appear to be older than the worship of personalized gods, I mean worship by our ancestors of Sun, Moon and Earth. The *Charm* for increasing the fertility of the fields, sometimes called *Æcerbot*, contains a pagan hymn to the sun and another to the earth. The hymn to the sun is introduced by the exhortation:

Turn to the east and bowing humbly nine times say then these words:

Eastwards I stand, for favours I pray
I pray the great Lord, I pray the mighty Prince
I pray the holy Warden of the heavenly kingdom
To earth I pray and to up-heaven . . .

Then turn three times sunwise and stretch yourself along the ground full length and say the litany there. . . .

Here is obvious sun-worship, no matter now obscured by Christian influence, just as the following embodies earth-worship:

Erce, Erce, Erce, Mother of Earth . . .
Hail to thee, Earth, mother of men!
Be fruitful in God's embrace,
Filled with food for the use of men.

Then take every kind of meal and have a loaf baked no bigger than the palm of your hand, having kneaded it with milk and holy water, and lay it under the first turned furrow.

This kind of hymn together with instruction in the ritual and sacrifice gives some insight into the ministrations of pagan priests.

Moon-worship is reflected in two charms from the *Herbarium* (8 and 10) where instructions are given to boil herbs in water 'when the moon is waning' and to wash the patient with the liquor; or to wreathe clove-wort with red thread round a lunatic's neck 'when the moon is waning, in April or early in October. Soon he will be healed.' There is little other literary attestation of moon-worship but there is no doubt of its existence: the laws of Canute expressly forbid moon-worship – with not much effect if observances which have lasted to the present day offer any clue. I am thinking of various ritual acts practised by some country gardeners who will not plant seeds except at a particular phase of the moon; and nearer home, I have vivid memories of my old grandmother who, to all intents and purposes a countrywoman of devoutly religious orthodoxy, every month without fail consulted the calendar for the rising of the new moon so that she could potter out into the garden (pince-nez in hand) to avoid a first sight of the bright deity through a window. To see the new moon first through glass (even spectacles) was sure to bring 'bad luck', in other words, such a misfortune was offensive to the deity who could be expected to react adversely.

We know from Old Saxon and Old Norse sources that the Sun and Moon came to be regarded respectively as a goddess and a god (not the other way about as in Classical myth); and additional proof that our forebears held such beliefs we can find in the names of the first two days of the week, Sunday and Monday. But as I have already said, there are elements in sun- and moon-worship which have even deeper roots than the regard for personalized gods. Such elements find expression in the various Bronze Age symbols representing the sun (like the four-spoked wheel or cross) and moon found carved on rocks in Scandinavia, as well as in sun chariots such as the one found at Trundholm in Denmark. Whether or to what extent such sun- and moon-worship was passed on to our North West European ancestors from the aborigines of the north whom they overran and absorbed, it is perhaps impossible now to determine.

The earliest important literary source written with the conscious intention of describing something of the Old English paganism is a section of the *De Temporum Ratione* by the Venerable Bede (AD 673–735). Bede says that the Anglo-Saxon heathen year began on 25 December; certain ceremonies, which he does not describe, gave what we now call Boxing Night the title of *modra nect* or 'mothers' night'. The last month of the old year and the first of the new were together called *Giuli* (modern Yule), a word whose meaning is uncertain. The second month of the new year was *Solmonath* when 'cakes were offered to their gods', says Bede. Most scholars reject this as an explanation of the name because no word *sol* meaning 'cakes' is known in Anglo-Saxon; but it seems to me that *sol* is an old word for 'sun' and that Bede's account is based on a genuine tradition. In fact, because *Solmonath* would coincide with what is now February when it is customary to begin the year's ploughing, and because of what we know of the baking of cakes to be placed in the first furrow according to the *Charm* to restore fertility to the land where both sun and earth are worshipped, it seems more than possible that Bede is remembering the ancient ritual of ploughing in the loaves.

The third and fourth months are said to be named after two goddesses called Hretha and Eostre (our Easter) though some scholars believe Bede was guilty of back formation here, that is to say, he constructed the names of these two in order to explain the names of the months; there is, however, no evidence to suggest such faking. *Thrimilci* was the name of the fifth month 'because cows were then milked three times a day'; a logical and practical name for May, when the flush of fresh green grass produces a corresponding flush of milk – a time of year which farmers with little means of overwintering stock and no concentrated cow-cake must have awaited with impatience and received with joy. The sixth and seventh months were together called *Litha*, an ancient name seemingly meaning 'moon'. *Weodmonath* was the 'weed month'; *Halegmonath* the 'holy month' or as Bede calls it 'month of offerings', which is an obvious indication of a heathen harvest festival. *Wintirfyllith* is connected by Bede with the appearance of the first full moon of winter – *winter-fyl-lith* 'winter-full-moon'; and November was *Blotmonath*, the blood month, 'because they sacrificed to their gods the animals which they were about to kill' – again a combination of religion and practical husbandry by primitive farmers who had not as yet found the means of keeping more than a small percentage of their flocks and herds alive during the winter.

These few remarks by Bede show us a people who of necessity fitted closely into the pattern of the changing year, who were of the earth and what grows in it, who breathed the farmy exhalations of cattle and sheep, who marked the passage of time according to the life-cycle of their stock and the growth of their plants or by the appropriate period for offerings to the gods, who drew on even deeper wells of religious feeling than the worship of personal gods, being conscious day and night of the sun in its majesty and the moon in its splendour: in fact, a people who were in a symbiotic relationship with mother earth and father sky: we, their descendants, no longer stand in such a relationship towards nature.

A comparison between ourselves and our ancestors in the light of their calendar will illuminate some of the dark corners (as we may think it) of their heathenism. Their roof was the sky with the sun by day and the moon by night: as for us, most of our heads are covered day and night by a home or office ceiling or a factory shed; their walls were the winds, ours are bricks and mortar; their floor was the earth carpeted with grass and crops, weeds and wild flowers, ours is concrete and tarmacadam; their measure of time was the seasons and the heavenly lights, ours is the alarm clock or the wireless 'pips'. Their food came not from processing plants, cans and deep-freeze cabinets but from their own fields and stock. Their clothes were not reach-me-downs at the end of a production line but rough homespun garments made by their own hands. And their success or failure in life depended not on the scientific application of knowledge, but on the gods and goddesses of the sky, earth and weather in combat with the demon giants of flood, fire, drought and pestilence. In other words, our forefathers of fifteen hundred years ago lived not what we call 'close to nature' but actually *involved* with nature: they were not creatures apart, different from the birds, plants or animals, but fitted into the natural cycle of synthesis and disintegration which any kind of

37

37 The dependence of the people of the time on largely subsistence farming which tied them closely to the land is indicated by such scenes as this one from the Utrecht Psalter.

civilization always modifies. Because they were involved with nature, with whom they had intimately to come to terms if they wanted to go on living, the Old English looked with awe on the life-giving sky and earth, on the death-dealing thunderstorm and winter. It is from the constant awareness of the living connection between man and the phenomenal world that the myths of our ancestors arise, that their gods are born. In spite of a millennium and a half of civilizing influences, we their descendants are occasionally able to slip into this same relationship with nature, as witness the following report of a terrifying thunderstorm from the *News Chronicle* for 30 August 1956:

> An 18-year-old sapper was killed when lightning struck six soldiers at Ash Ranges, near Aldershot, yesterday. . . . The N.C.O. in charge, Sergeant William Kendrick, said: 'It looked as if they had been in action. There was a terrific bang. Everything went black and it seemed as though someone was trying to hammer us into the ground.'

Is there any wonder that the Old English looked on the thunderstorm as the great god Thunor whose hammer was the thunderbolt? For the attitude of Sergeant Kendrick (perhaps only for a few seconds) is plainly shown by his words to have been the same as our pagan ancestors', namely, that the demonic and the divine were immanent in nature.

There are written proofs that the pagan English had temples in which they housed images of the gods they wished to praise and appease. Bede quotes a letter (dated 17 June 601) written by Pope Gregory the Great to Abbot Mellitus on the departure of the Abbot for England:

> When (by God's help) you come to our most reverend brother, Bishop Augustine [in Kent], I want you to tell him how earnestly I have been pondering over the affairs of the English: I have come to the conclusion that the temples of the idols in England should not on any account be destroyed. Augustine must smash the idols, but the temples themselves should be sprinkled with holy water and altars set up in them in which relics are to be

enclosed. For we ought to take advantage of well-built temples by purifying them from devil-worship and dedicating them to the service of the true God. In this way, I hope the people (seeing their temples are not destroyed) will leave their idolatry and yet continue to frequent the places as formerly, so coming to know and revere the true God. And since the sacrifice of many oxen to devils is their custom, some other rite ought to be solemnized in its place such as a Day of Dedication or Festivals for the holy martyrs whose relics are there enshrined. On such high days the people might well build themselves shelters of boughs round about the churches that were once temples and celebrate the occasion with pious feasting. They must no more sacrifice animals to the Devil, but they may kill them for food to the glory of God while giving thanks for his bounty to the provider of all gifts.

Bede himself knew an unbroken tradition of at least one heathen temple seen by King Aldwulf of East Anglia 'who lived into our own times' and who testified 'that this temple was still standing in his day, and that he had seen it when a boy'. It had belonged to Aldwulf's predecessor King Redwald who had been baptized in Kent but who (says Bede) 'like the ancient Samaritans, tried to serve both Christ and the old gods, having in one and the same temple an altar for the holy sacrifice of Christ alongside an altar on which victims were offered to devils'. That the idols were actual representations of gods in human shape is borne out by a letter from Pope Boniface to King Edwin of Northumbria (written *c.* 625). Boniface urges Edwin to accept Christianity and leave the old heathen ways; he writes:

> The profound guilt of those who wilfully adhere to insidious superstition and the worship of idols is openly shown in the damnable images they adore. The Psalmist says of such, 'All the heathen gods are devils; it is the Lord who made the heavens.' And again, 'They have ears and hear not; they have noses and are not able to smell; they have hands and cannot feel; they have feet and do not walk. Therefore, those who make them are like them, as are all who put trust and confidence in them.' How can such stocks and stones have power to assist you when they are made to order from perishable materials by the labour of your own subjects and journeymen? Even their lifeless resemblance to human form is solely due to man's workmanship.

King Edwin was, of course, converted; and as Christianity began properly to take hold, kings went out of their way to enact laws which had the suppression of heathenism as their aim. On the expectancy of there being no smoke without fire one may confidently believe that the old gods had their adherents quite up to the time of the Norman Conquest, for we find in the laws of Canute: '5. Of Heathenism. And we strictly forbid all heathenism. It is heathen for a man to worship idols, that is, to worship heathen gods, and the sun or moon, fire or flood, water wells or stones, or any kind of wood-trees, or practice witchcraft, or contrive murder by sorcery.' I have already mentioned relics of moon-worship down to the present, and as for a memory of the worship of wells one need go no further today than Castleton or Bakewell in Derbyshire – not even as far as Lourdes.

We may conclude, then, that the Angles, Saxons and Jutes were practising heathens during their first five generations in England and that
the evidence of their heathenism is not so scanty as some historians
would have us believe. They worshipped at least four divinities, Woden,
Thunor, Tiw and Frig, they had temples, images of the gods and priests.
The temples (like their houses) were wooden-framed and so have perished,
but they appear to have been simple rectangular ridge-roofed structures
set up in forest clearings possibly in association with sacred groves or a
venerated tree and a holy well. Inside the temple was a sanctum with an
altar and a likeness of one or more gods. If ancient Norse and Icelandic
fanes offer a parallel, then the Old English temple furniture included a
gold ring upon which oaths were sworn, a bowl for catching the blood
of sacrificed animals and a bunch of twigs for splattering the blood over
worshippers in the same way as holy water is asperged upon devout
Catholics. There is reason to believe that the priests combined in some
cases their religious role with that of secular chief or headman of a district.
Religious rites followed the changing year with sacrifices of animals
which were eaten at ritual feasts: the rites alternated as pleas for favours
and thanks for favours received. It is reasonable to suppose that where
very existence depended upon a bounteous earth and a fertilizing sky,
these two were in the forefront of men's minds in religious matters. I shall
argue that this was the case with the Old English no matter what the
current name for the two great providers happened to be.

For the present, then, we may believe that our forefathers of fifteen
hundred years ago were devout heathens who believed that their very
lives depended on their devotion. And, for that matter, who is to say
that they were mistaken?

38 One leaf of the two which have survived from a book-length Anglo-Saxon epic poem *Waldere*. The vellum pages, with sixty complete lines of verse, had been used as stiffening in the binding of a work owned by the Royal Library, Copenhagen. They were discovered in 1860 and found to mention not only Wayland but his son Widia by Beadohild, and Beadohild's father King Nidhad who had had Wayland hamstrung (see lines 7 and 8). The importance of these references is that they are purely allusive, proving beyond doubt that the Anglo-Saxon audience for whom *Waldere* was intended knew all the circumstances of the Wayland myth.

Chapter Four
WYRD

We have to admit that our ancestors were heathen when they first came to Britain. But, having been conditioned by thirteen hundred years of Christianity, we are apt to forget that even heathens have gods together with some description of how the world began, how man was created and what happens to him after death. Many heathen mythologies go on to relate how the world itself will end.

There are reasons for believing that Anglo-Saxon mythology made mention of all these things.

So far as they accept a god or gods and a mythology, the present-day descendants of the Anglo-Saxons have borrowed from the Jews. The Jews came to be uncompromising believers in one god, they were mono-theists. Our own ancestors were polytheists, believing in a number of gods, a family of them with father and mother, sons and daughters. One may suspect that there is still more than a trace of polytheism in the beliefs of the modern English Christian (old racial habits of thought die hard), and especially the Roman Catholic Christian: for the pantheon includes God the Father, God the Son, the Holy Ghost, the Divine Mother and any number of wonder-working saints.

The formal conversion of the English to Christianity began when Augustine landed in Thanet a little more than a hundred years after the first Angles, Saxons and Jutes had begun to settle here. Augustine's mission to convert them started in the year AD 597. At this time the English formed an island outpost of heathendom, for they were practi-cally surrounded by Christian peoples in the Celts of Cornwall, Wales, Ireland and Scotland and the Franks across the Channel. When the heathen king of Kent, Ethelbert, heard of Augustine's landing with some forty companions he sent orders for them not to move off Thanet. King Ethelbert himself may be said to have had his right foot planted firmly on the straight and narrow path already, since for nine years he had been married to Bertha, a daughter of Charibert of Paris and a Christian. Bertha's marriage contract had stipulated that she be allowed to remain a practising Christian and to have with her in Ethelbert's court Bishop Liudhard of the Franks. It is perhaps obvious that no man could have Christianity in bed and at breakfast for nine years without being affected.

Nevertheless, according to what appears to be a genuine tradition, King Ethelbert consented to meet the stranger monks only under the open sky because he was afraid of their magic. Or should we say because he wished to meet them in the presence of the old Sky Father? Whatever it was, he was soon convinced that they were not magicians and gave the missionaries his support. And who could have been more surprised than the tonsured father who had led his procession of singing followers to greet the King: Ethelbert seated in a chair, and they walking behind a raised silver cross and a likeness of the Saviour painted on a board? For Augustine had turned back once in his mission, having been frightened by gossip of the barbarous practices of the fierce English. Instead of barbarity, King Ethelbert gave Augustine supplies, a dwelling in Canterbury and permission to preach. He himself was baptized, his lead being followed by his thanes and ordinary subjects, so that Augustine could claim that 10,000 men of Kent had been baptized by the end of the first year of his mission.

Christianity spread to the other kingdoms of Anglo-Saxon England, to Northumbria, to Mercia, to Wessex, and in spite of backslidings and fairly frequent returns to paganism by influential kings, the country could claim to be Christian by the time of the Synod of Whitby in the year 664.

In those days society knew something of a closed shop as stringent as any modern one with every man from the king downwards filling his appointed place and doing his ordained task not at the behest of a shop steward but (in the heathen period) of Wyrd or Destiny, and (in Christian times) of God himself. With the institution of a new class of society, namely the Christian priests and bishops whose business was with words and ideas, there grew up a new trade, that of books. This new trade of written literature remained for centuries in the hands of priests and their adherents and wholly under the jurisdiction of the Church. Formerly, the heathen Angles, Saxons and Jutes had cultivated a flourishing pagan *spoken* literature which depended for its life and growth on a well-defined alliterative verse-form easier than prose to memorize and on *gleomen* and *scops*, wandering minstrels or poets attached to the household of a great man, having prodigious memories as well as creative powers of their own. But the poets were the one exception to every man to his trade; they might well hand the harp to their nearest lay neighbour at the festive board to continue singing while they themselves quaffed beer or mead to slake their fiery throats.

It is not easy for us after some years of compulsory 'education', free libraries, cheap newspapers and – latterly – cinema, radio and television to imagine a people whose memories were muscular, supple, in training and therefore quick to learn, capacious and extraordinarily retentive. At the turn of the sixth century in England it was the mark of the magician to be able to write, for writing meant the cutting or scratching of runes on stone, bone or metal, and the purpose of rune-risting was more often than not to do with soothsaying or sorcery. But our illiterate ancestors did have codes of law, they did have histories, sagas and myths which

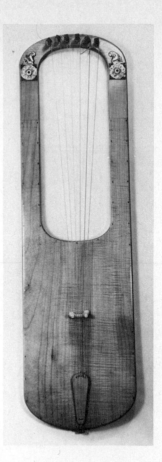

39 Originally reconstructed
as a harp, the fragments of a
musical instrument from
Sutton Hoo are now seen to
have been a lyre.

(like their mile-long family trees) were passed from ear to tongue, from
one generation to another, often in rhythmical form to give the memory
at least a little support. A curse of modern society is that it has a high
mortality rate in poets: they get mashed up in the machinery. The Old
English, on the other hand, held poets in high esteem with priests and
kings. Great respect was paid to the art of 'finding sayings rightly bound',
that is, in alliterative verse, and it was a matter at least for private shame
to have to leave the feast (as Cædmon at first was wont to do) before the
'glee-wood', the harp passing from hand to hand, reached you because   39
you were unable to sing. Kings as well as commoners sang: we are told in
Beowulf that Hrothgar, lord of the Danes

> the glee-wood touched
> the harp's sweet note awoke; and now a song intoned,
> both sooth and sad; now the great-hearted king
> told well a wondrous tale.

The aristocracy, kings and thanes, maintained 'shapers' or 'makers' of
verse (for that is what *scop* stands for) at their courts, while the *gleoman*,
or gleeman, wandered far and wide among men with his harp. In fact,
one of our earliest poems is called *Widsith*, 'the Far Traveller', from its

maker who tells how he visited all the North West European and other people of the Continent, not to mention the Medes, Persians and Jews.

Of course, *Widsith* is not the record of the actual wanderings of a real glee-man. A minstrel who claimed to have been at the court of Ermanric (who died AD 375) could not have been in Italy with Alfwine (who invaded that country in 568). *Widsith* the poem is a glorification of the class to which Widsith the poet belonged:

> Thus wandering, the minstrels travel as chance will have it through the lands of many different peoples. Always they are bound to come across, in the north or the south, some person who is touched by their song and is generous with his gifts, who will increase his reputation in front of his henchmen showing his nobility of spirit before worldly things pass away, the light and the life. He who works for his own good name will be rewarded on earth by a strong and steady fame.

The situation is admirably summed up by Bernhard ten Brink who said:

> herein lies the essential difference between that age and our own; the result of poetical activity was not the property and not the production of a single person, but of the community. The work of the individual singer endured only as long as its delivery lasted. He gained personal distinction only as a virtuoso. The permanent elements of what he presented, the material, the ideas, even the style and metre, already existed. The work of the singer was only a ripple in the stream of national poetry. Who can say how much the individual contributed to it, or where in his poetical recitation memory ceased and creative impulse began! In any case the work of the individual lived on only as the ideal possession of the aggregate body of the people, and it soon lost the stamp of originality.

What is important for us to realize is that while minstrels continued down the ages to wander and sing, the subject of which they treated could not be forgotten or entirely stamped out by proselytizing clerics. And as regards the subject-matter, if we are to judge from the literary relics of the blood relations of the Old English, that is to say from the literature of the ancient Scandinavian peoples and even further back, from the works of others of the Indo-European knot of peoples, of the Hindus, Greeks and Romans, then two subjects were exploited: gods and heroes.

After the English were converted, Christian poets still sang about gods and heroes, but (as frequently happens in such cases) the gods of the old religion became the devils of the new, while Jesus Christ is referred to as 'the young hero', as in the Anglo-Saxon poem called the *Dream of the Rood*.

But the broader effect is for the old gods to be dropped almost completely from the new written literature: their names are suppressed, though (as I shall suggest) their stories sometimes live on in a Christian setting. Like ancient ruins which tease the curiosity of the beholder, or like fossils, the remains of these deities still lie about us. As we have seen, they survive in place-names, or they live on in the one spot calculated to

40 First leaf of the *Beowulf* manuscript, an epic poem of book length miraculously preserved from fire, flood and time; translated it reads:

Lo! haven't we all heard of the might of the Danish Spear-kings, how in the days of yore those princes wrought heroic deeds!

Time and time again, Scyld Scefing captured the towns of mead-merry warriors, scores of tribes: he brought terror to the jarls. Discovered at first in want and hunger, his comfort ever afterwards increased and he grew up under the open skies to such worship and worth that all neighbouring peoples over the whale's way acknowledged his rule and rendered him tribute. That was a good king! Next, he was blessed with a son in his court whom God sent as a solace to his people, for He understood their sufferings when a longsome while they had had no king: in compensation the Frey of Life, the Ruler of Glory gave him this honour in the world. Beowulf Scyld's son was renowned not only in Scania but his fame spread afar. So may a young man bring about good with splendid gifts in his father's . . .

escape our notice, that is to say under our very noses in the names of the days of the week – Sunday, Monday, Tuesday, Wednesday, Thursday and Friday. Or again, both pagan deities and myths are remembered in folklore and fairy-tale with their stories of Wayland Smith, witches on broomsticks and the Wild Rider who is really Woden in disguise. Or yet again, in works of art like the Franks Casket already described, o: in pictured plaques on helmets or the decoration of shoulder-clasps, buckles and purse-tops such as those dug up at Sutton Hoo.

Much as we have suffered from the conscious effort to suppress the old mythology in literature, our loss was made the greater at the time of the Reformation in England when hundreds and thousands of books and manuscripts were lost or destroyed on the libraries of abbeys and monasteries being flung out of doors. John Bale in his preface to *Leland's Laboryouse Journey* printed at London in 1549 says that those who bought the monasteries reserved the books, some to scour their candlesticks, some to scrub their boots, some for even more ignoble uses, some they sold to the grocers and soap-sellers, and some they sent overseas to the bookbinders, not in small numbers but at times whole shipsful, to the wonderment of foreign nations. That John Bale was not exaggerating is suggested first by the fact that most of such Anglo-Saxon poetry as has survived is contained in only *four* manuscript books, and secondly by the circumstances (already remarked on) of the accidental discovery in Denmark of a fragment of an Anglo-Saxon epic known as *Waldere*. It happened like this: on 12 January 1860, Professor E. C. Werlauff, Chief Librarian of the National Library, Copenhagen 'was engaged in sorting some bundles of papers, parchment leaves, and fragments, mostly taken from books, or book backs, which had not hitherto been arranged. While thus occupied, he lighted upon two vellum leaves of great antiquity, and bearing an Old English text.' How are the mighty fallen! Sixty lines – this was all that was left of *Waldere*, an epic originally (we may suspect) as long as *Beowulf* which contains over three thousand lines or more words than a Shakespearean play.

One result of such losses is that to attempt a reconstruction of the ancient English mythology is to engage in a piece of detective work whose clues lie far-scattered, often hidden and liable to suggest conclusions which at best are tentative and may never be capable of proof. But the chase need not be dull and on the contrary may be exciting.

Take the Anglo-Saxon poem just mentioned, *Beowulf*: this is the tale of a warrior-prince who, in his full youth and vigour, wrestled with an ape-like monster who for years had been lugging off by night ten or twenty at a time the retainers of the Danish King Hrothgar. Young Beowulf sailed from Sweden to Denmark and in the blackness of Hrothgar's sleeping hall awaited the coming of the ogre Grendel from the gloomy moor: when the monster broke in, the warrior grappled with him. Then the chairs and benches in the hall were overturned and smashed to flinders. Grendel quickly understood that for the first time in his life he had met his match, and he tried to drag his opponent to the hall door. Beowulf grimly held back and when at last the monster succeeded in

41 The medieval barn at Tisbury, a direct descendant of the halls of the Anglo-Saxon kings and nobles. The great hall called 'Heorot' in *Beowulf* was built after this fashion; there, in the dead of night, as the warriors slept, came the monster Grendel only to have his arm wrenched from its socket by the young Beowulf.

breaking out into the fading starlight he finally wrenched with such a panic that his massive arm was torn like a molar from its bloody socket and left in Beowulf's grasp. The doomed Grendel staggered off to the moor leaving in the morning twilight a wet, black trail behind him.

The poem goes on to relate the vengeance of Grendel's mother, an ogress, and how after diving down into the sink-hole of a lonely and fearsome tarn, Beowulf killed her in an underground cave. In his later life, Beowulf became king of his people and in saving them from the attacks of a fire-breathing dragon was himself destroyed. His grateful subjects burnt his body on a pyre, later heaping a huge mound of stones and earth over the ashes.

It is quite by chance that this wonderful old epic has escaped the fate of *Waldere*, or worse; for, having evaded the ravages of time and the tearing up wholesale of libraries at the Dissolution of the Monasteries, the unique manuscript came within a whiff of destruction when Ashburnham House caught fire in 1731. At the time, *Beowulf* formed part of the library of Sir Thomas Cotton, and its vellum pages were near enough to cinders for some of the edges to be scorched and made brittle so that they have chipped away, and with the lost fragments part of the text has gone too. About the end of the eighteenth century Thorkelin, an Icelander, came to England, copied the manuscript himself and caused another copy to be made. He spent years preparing an edition only to have his translation and notes annihilated by, of all people, Admiral Nelson: for most of Thorkelin's material went up in smoke when the English bombarded Copenhagen in 1807. But the copy of *Beowulf* did escape and the Icelander's edition appeared at last in 1815.

The three thousand lines of alliterating verse which go to make up *Beowulf* were being composed in the north of England or East Anglia about AD 650, at a time when the conversion of the English to Christianity was hardly complete. It was, in fact, barely two hundred years since the first colonizing Angles, Saxons and Jutes had set foot in Britain. But while the conscious intention of the poem is Christian, God being mentioned on average every sixty lines or so, the remarkable fact is that the setting is quite pagan and foreign and none of the characters is English. There is reliable history in *Beowulf*, but it is not English history: it is a memory of people who lived and events which took place on the Continent, the background being Denmark and the southern parts of the Scandinavian Peninsula. Some of the continental history is presented in fairly involved detail; if it could be remembered and recorded a couple of hundred years after it had taken place then it is obvious that, had he wanted to do so, the *Beowulf* poet could far more easily have recorded the pagan myths then recently supplanted by Christianity. That he did not, must be regarded as a deliberate act. Nevertheless, the poet could not entirely suppress all pagan folk-memory and unwittingly he left a number of clues to the old mythology scattered throughout his poem.

We may start with a clue to a fundamental idea not only of Old English mythology, but of Indo-European myth generally: this idea is that of an all-powerful Fate or Destiny. The name of this Fate in Old English was

Wyrd, who was originally pictured as a woman, a dread omnipotent personality to whom even the gods were subject.

The word 'wyrd' occurs nine times in *Beowulf* with the meaning 'omnipotent fate or destiny'; but there is confusion in the mind of the poet, for he accepts elsewhere in his poem the omnipotence of the Christian God too. Two omnipotent powers cannot exist together, so the line of development is clear: one or other must give up its position. Such a move may be effected in two ways; either God or Wyrd will be effaced and forgotten, or, since the Christian religion is gaining the upper hand at this time, before long God and Wyrd will be identified with each other, Wyrd becoming an attribute of God, his Providence. This is actually what did take place, but for some time during the transition period Wyrd is remembered in Old English writings as all-powerful with the Christian God Himself subject to her power.

In spite of what modern writers such as Miss Dorothy Whitelock would have us believe, this truly remarkable state of affairs must be inferred from, for instance, some of the earliest Anglo-Saxon verse such as the *Gnomic Poems* and the *Dream of the Rood*.

The *Gnomic Poems* show verse in a very early form: they consist of sententious sayings which often appear to be unrelated to each other. But when we find two such statements as the following occurring in one breath: 'the glories of Christ are great; Wyrd is strongest of all', one can only conclude that the poet was remembering his old myths. This is not an isolated instance; it is repeated even more graphically in the *Rood*. At the crucifixion, after describing Christ's hanging on the cross and his wounding with nails, the Rood says, 'I was dripping with blood shed from the Man's side after he had given up the ghost', and most significantly, immediately afterwards, 'I have endured many terrible Wyrds upon the hill' – *feala ic on tham beorge gebiden hæbbe wrathra wyrda.* Modern translators usually render the word *Wyrds* as 'trials' or 'experiences'; but when it comes, as it does, immediately on the mention of Christ's death, it is reasonable to suppose that the poet was remembering the old power wielded by Wyrd over the gods. A similar example is repeated at lines 72 ff. of the *Rood*: 'the corpse grew cold, that fair house of the soul. Then men began to fell us to the ground: that was a terrible Wyrd!'

The unique manuscript of the *Dream of the Rood* is comparatively late, being dated about A D 1000. Part of the poem itself (from line 78 onwards) appears to have been added round about this time, but the rest is much earlier. We have certain proof of this from having found quotations from it cut in runes on the celebrated cross at Ruthwell in Dumfriesshire. And the Ruthwell Cross is judged by most recent authorities to have been carved about the year A D 700, so that the *Dream of the Rood* must be almost as old as *Beowulf*. It is from the original part of the *Rood* that the evidence I have given above is drawn.

Nevertheless, the uncertainty with which our ancestors thought about Wyrd in the transition period before she became God's Providence is reflected in another quotation from *Beowulf*, a quotation which, even as it tends to identify Wyrd with the Christian God, remembers most clearly

103

104, 105

the pagan goddess spinning the thread of life. I am thinking of line 696 of *Beowulf*, where we read 'the Lord gave the people of the Weders webs to speed them in their battles'. To the uninitiated this sentence is almost without meaning, even when we realize that 'webs' are woven cloths. The meaning would have been obvious if for instance the sentence had run 'the Lord gave the people of the Weders better bows and arrows to speed them in their battles'. The explanation of the original is that the poet has made a metaphor from the old pagan conception of Wyrd as Fate. Wyrd was originally one of three sisters, the Fatal Sisters, who were concerned with the spinning of a thread or the weaving of a cloth which represented the lives of men. In this case the *Beowulf* poet has given a pale cast of Christianity to a purely heathen thought by imagining God as the weaver. A couple of centuries after this, Christian men no longer regarded God as being subject to Wyrd: the wheel has turned full circle and Wyrd is identified with or subject to God or regarded as one of his attributes; for King Alfred the Great, writing about the year 888, says in his translation of Boethius' *De Consolatione Philosophiae*, 'What we call Wyrd is really the work of God about which He is busy every day' – *Ac thæt thæt we Wyrd hatath, thæt bith Godes weorc thæt he ælce dæg wyrceth.*

Miss Dorothy Whitelock, in *The Beginnings of English Society*, is convinced that though there are Old English references where some degree of personification of fate is present

> such as 'the creation of the fates changes the world under the heavens' or 'woven by the decrees of fate' [nevertheless she doubts] if these are more than figures of speech by the times the poems were composed. If they are inherited from a heathen past, they may indicate that men then believed in a goddess who wove their destiny, but the poet who says 'to him the Lord granted the webs of victory' is unconscious of a heathen implication in his phrase.

Such phrases as Miss Whitelock quotes may have become clichés by the time we meet them, but this development does not invalidate the contention that our ancestors did once believe in a Fate who wove their destinies. The same words connected with both 'weaving' and 'destiny' or 'fortune' make it certain that the Old English had believed in such a dread personage. Take, for example, the Old English phrase *me thæt wyrd gewæf* – 'fate wove me that destiny' and compare the word *gewæf* 'wove' with its cognate O.E. *gewif* meaning 'fortune'; or O.E. *eaden* and *ead* meaning 'wealth, riches, fortune', the basic sense of which appears in the related Lithuanian word *audmi* 'I weave'.

In actual fact, the idea of Wyrd as one of three sisters who weave men's fates is kept alive long after the conversion to Christianity. In written works of the Old English period the thought of Wyrd as a goddess was consciously played down by monkish writers and copyists. That is why such phrases as those quoted above have tended to become meaningless clichés. But the idea of the three pagan Fates lived long in oral tradition, for centuries in fact, until it exploded into most dramatic representation in 1605 in the three 'Weird Sisters' of Shakespeare's *Macbeth*. That this was no isolated flight of fancy nor even a refurbishing of Classical myth by one who knew a little Latin if less Greek is indicated by other references over the years intervening between Ethelbert of Kent and Elizabeth of England. For instance, the Latin name of the three Fates, 'Parcae', appears as 'Wyrde' in the Corpus Gloss (Hessels) about AD 725; then about 1385 Chaucer in the *Legend of Good Women* (*Hypermnestra* 19) is writing of

> the Werdys that we clepyn Destiné;

and about 1450 in the *Court of Love* we read

> I mene the three of fatall destiné
> that be our Werdes;

and so on to *Macbeth*. It would be perverse not to believe that what Shakespeare wrote was the flowering of a seed perennial in the folk-mind. But it is instructive to observe that according to the *New English Dictionary* the word 'wyrd'

> is common in Old English but wanting in Middle English until *c.* 1300, and then occurs chiefly in northern texts, though employed by Chaucer, Gower and Langland.

It now becomes apparent that after the development noted in Alfred's Boethius when Wyrd had been made subject to the Christian God, the Church (controlling literature) suppressed the pagan word in writing as well as the idea. That both word and idea only went underground (or would 'faded into thin air' be a better metaphor?) and lived on secretly upon the lips of gleemen and the laity is proved by their reappearance in the secular literature of the later Middle Ages after three hundred years of being unrecorded.

How, over such a long period, had the pagan conception submitted to alteration? A study of what Shakespeare has to say on the subject will soon tell us: he portrays three witches who are referred to in Macbeth's letter to his wife as 'weird sisters'; these sisters foretell the future and are able to influence what is to come to pass; they are dreadful in aspect and connected with darkness – 'How now, you secret, black, and midnight hags!'; they work their spells in a cavern about a circular cauldron; they seem to be concerned with battles, for the opening words of *Macbeth* run

FIRST WITCH: When shall we three meet again
              In thunder, lightning, or in rain?
SECOND WITCH: When the hurlyburly's done,
              When the battle's lost and won.

Here, in fact, we have all except one of the main attributes of the ancient Indo-European Fates together with the addition of what appears to be a purely North West European development, namely, the belief that the three sisters were specially concerned to give defeat or victory in battle: this was what the *Beowulf* poet was remembering when he said 'the Lord gave the people of the Weders webs to speed them in their battles'. But apart from the ideas of the omnipotence of Wyrd over the destinies of gods and men, and the memory of her power to influence the course of battle, our Old English literature does not record the Indo-European conceptions revived in *Macbeth*. Yet we must believe that the pagan Anglo-Saxons knew these conceptions, partly because of the clues in Old English literature already discussed, partly because of their reappearance in English literature as late as the sixteenth century and partly because we find them recorded in the literature of a closely related people – the Icelanders.

Long after the English had become Christians, the Icelanders were still writing down the ancient pagan beliefs about the Fates. The people of Iceland called Wyrd by the name Urdr (a sound change peculiar to the Norse peoples had resulted in the initial *w* being lost from certain words of which Urdr is an example); in Old Saxon she is Wurd and in Old High German, Wurt. All these forms of the name derive from the same word, an ancient verb meaning 'to become', which we still find fossilized in such archaic English phrases as 'woe worth'. The Icelanders called Urdr's two sisters Verdandi and Skuld; these three names together being equivalent to Past, Present and Future. Collectively, the sisters were known as the Nornir and they were said to dwell in heaven by the side of a well over which stands one of the massive roots of the mighty World Ash Tree called Yggdrasill. Every day the Norns took water from the well and, mixing it with clay from the banks, pasted the Ash Tree root to prevent its limbs from withering or rotting. For, according to the Icelandic storyteller, the water of the well of Urdr is so holy that all things which dip into it become as white as the film which shines within the shell of an egg.

We may return for a few moments to the Elizabethan traditions about the 'weird sisters' to record a significant connection between them also and a tree which, as far as I am aware, has not been noticed before. Shakespeare used as a source for the three sisters Holinshed's *Chronicles* where we read:

> It fortuned as Makbeth and Banquho iournied towards Fores, where the king then laie, they went sporting by the waie togither without other companie, saue onelie themselues, passing thorough the woods and fields, when suddenlie in the middest of a laund, there met them three women in strange and wild apparell, resembling creatures of elder world, whome when they attentiuelie beheld, woondering much at the sight, the first of them spake and said: '*All haile, Makbeth, thane of Glammis!*' (for he had latelie entered into that dignitie and office by the death of his father Sinell). The second of them said: '*Haile, Makbeth, thane of Cawder!*' But the third said: '*All haile, Makbeth, that heereafter shall be king of Scotland!*'

Now, on page 243 of the first edition of Holinshed's *Chronicles* there is a woodcut of this episode, but as Dover Wilson says in his edition of *Macbeth*, 'It is certainly noteworthy that the draughtsman dresses the Sisters as great (Elizabethan) ladies and represents the scene as a barren heath, ignoring Holinshed's express words in both particulars.' This

42

42 The Weird Sisters. This woodcut from the first edition of Holinshed's *Chronicles* is significant for including a flourishing tree as the centre-piece of a landscape which according to Shakespeare's *Macbeth* is a 'blasted heath'. There can be no doubt that the three sisters are the three northern Fates, the Norns, in another guise. The name Weird is cognate with the Norse name of the first sister, Urd. The supposition is that the tree in the woodcut may well be a memory of the World Ash Yggdrasill under one of whose roots the Norns had their abode (*see also* Ill. 107 showing the temple of Uppsala with a tree and a well).

suggests that the artist knew of an independent tradition concerning the weird sisters, a tradition which also included a tree. For the very centre-piece of his otherwise blasted heath is a huge and flourishing tree by which the sisters stand. Is it too much to suppose that here is a memory of Yggdrasill? Holinshed himself is speaking of personages who were more than the poor old human hags regarded as witches, as we may gather from his phrase 'creatures of elder world' where 'elder' means the same as 'eldritch', that is, weird or ghostly: indeed, he later supposes they might have been the 'goddesses of destinie'. And their connection with past, present and future is expressly emphasized with one sister speaking of what has already happened, the second of what is present (though unknown to Macbeth) and the third with what is to come.

It is certain, not only from the mention of webs in *Beowulf* but also from the Greek parallel of the Moirai or Fates, that Urdr (that is to say, our Wyrd) and her sisters were originally thought of as spinners. The names of the Greek Fates were Clotho (who spun), Lachesis (who measured the thread) and Atropos (who snapped or cut the thread and so ended man's life). According to the old view, the Moirai were the daughters of Night; they lived in heaven in a cave by a pool whose white water gushed from the cave. This, says Kerényi in his *Gods of the Greeks*, is a clear image of moonlight. The name *moira* means 'part' and 'their number, so the Orphists claim, correspond to the "parts" of the moon; and that is why Orpheus sings of the "Moirai in white raiment".'

The Romans called the Fates 'Parcae', which is a word connected with the Latin verb *parere* meaning 'to bring forth' and so links the sisters with man's birth and life. The individual Latin names of the three sisters were Nona, Decima and Morta. The first two presided over different months of birth (the names connect with words meaning 'nine' and 'ten') and the last ruled death.

In spite of the widespread separation of the various Indo-European peoples and of such changes in their speech as to make one foreign to the other, the Greeks, Romans and North West Europeans have individually retained the basic ideas concerning the Fates. It is evident that the conception of the three Fates goes back to Indo-European times and that the ancestresses of Wyrd, the Norns, the Parcae and the Moirai were three all-powerful figures of at least six thousand years ago.

It is instructive to draw up a chart by which we can see at a glance the information in each source concerning the three Fates:

	Greek	Roman	Old Norse	Old English	Shakespeare and Holinshed
Number	3	3	3	?	3
Collective names	Moirai	Parcae	Nornir	?	Weird Sisters
Individual names	Clotho Lachesis Atropos	Nona Decima Morta	Urdr Verdandi Skuld	Wyrd ? ?	? ? ?
Work: metaphorical	Spinners	Spinners	Spinners	Spinners	?
Work: real	Controlling men's fates	Controlling men's fates	Controlling men's fates	Controlling men's fates	Controlling men's fates
Abode	Cave and pool	?	Cave, well and tree	? ?	Cavern and cauldron (and tree?)
Origin	Daughters of Night	?	?	?	'Secret, black, and midnight hags'; 'Creatures of elder world'; 'Goddesses of destinie'

We see that because all the other sources except the Old English have *three* Fates (including Shakespeare and Holinshed who are reproducing an Old English tradition not now extant in Anglo-Saxon) our fore-fathers must have known about three Fates. Their collective name has been lost to English tradition, and apart from Wyrd, so have their individual names. On the analogy of Old Norse, the two sisters of Wyrd ought to be called Weorthend and Sculd: but there is no evidence to support such a conclusion. However, I would venture to suggest that the middle sister's name may have been known to the Anglo-Saxons as Metod. This is a word found only as a synonym of the Christian God in extant writings, and is taken to be a masculine noun, but this is no real bar to my sugges-tion. The usual translation of Metod is 'Creator' yet its literal meaning is 'measurer', the word being connected with the modern verb 'to mete out'. There is at least a suspicion that Metod was a pagan name for one of the Fates, the one who measured out the thread of life, the name being later transferred to the Christian God. This contention is supported by Bosworth on page 165 of his *Anglo-Saxon and English Dictionary* under the entry 'Metan'.

Although evidence of the origin and abode of Wyrd and her sisters is lacking in Old English, nevertheless the evidence of Greek, Old Norse and Elizabethan sources confirms the connection of the Fates with a cavern, a well and night. From this we might go on to ask: What *were* they? What was their essence? What were they an emblem of? It is pretty conclusive that three all-powerful sisters, Daughters of Night, who lived in a cave by a round, white well, and whose names were associated with the division of time, had much in common with the phases of the moon, crescent, full and waning – especially the phases of the moon as an ancient measure of time – that same moon which gave its name to one of the North West European peoples' units of time which we still call 'month'.

The importance of this identification cannot be exaggerated for (as we shall see) it affords an explanation of what to us appears inexplicable, namely, that the Old English should have regarded the all-powerful God as being subject to Fate. But before seeking this explanation we ought to answer the question: Who was god?

Chapter Five
WHO WAS GOD?

Many religions refer to god as the Father; others are content to have a goddess Mother.

The knowledge of paternity is usually brought to a child's notice from the time it begins to say 'Daddy', and in modern society the explanation follows at puberty or thereabouts.

The Indo-Europeans were wise children some six thousand years ago. They knew their own fathers; or at least, they knew that a child had to have a father. This matter of paternity is by no means self-evident, as we may well understand when we consider the widespread religious belief in the god who is born fatherless, whose mother is extolled as a virgin. Even today, the Australian aborigines of the Outback deny any part played by the male in the procreation of children; the Trobriand Islanders have no word in their language for *father* because they recognize no such idea. The Trobrianders are willing to accept sexual intercourse as a pleasurable occupation complete in itself – a labour of love; a belief not half as unlikely as that once held among maidens in this country that being kissed by a young man would make them pregnant.

Motherhood is obvious, for anybody knows where the baby comes from. But the primitive peoples of millennia ago were arguing from the position of Trobrianders and Blackfellows when they postulated a Divine Family consisting of a virgin mother and her son. Our Indo-European ancestors had moved on beyond this stage of knowledge, for while they based their religious conceptions on the family, it was a family of which the head was a father: and this father was identified with the sky.

As far as we know, nobody ever wrote down the name of the Indo-European Sky Father; but from forms found in the languages which developed from Indo-European we can construct the Sky Father's name with tolerable certainty. It was either Djevs or Deivos.

Some examples of the form taken by the name in languages descended from the parent tongue are Sanskrit Dyaus, Greek Zeus and Latin Jovis. Often the local word for 'father' is tacked on the end of these names as Dyauspitar, Zeuspater and Jupiter. The meaning of Djevs and Deivos was 'resplendent' or 'shining', that is to say the name covered the most

43 Purse-top and clasps from the Sutton Hoo treasure (*see* Ills. 55 and 95).

striking and beneficent attribute of the sky: so the ancient Djevs is taken to be the Sky Father.

Since the Indians, Greeks and Romans all remembered the Sky Father it would be odd if our own North West European ancestors did not, for he can be shown to be the original Indo-European chief god, and the North West Europeans were an important branch of the Indo-European-speaking tribes. Does his name then appear in the oral or literary remains of our forefathers? Let me say bluntly (for authorities in the past have doubted it) that the answer is 'yes' and that the putative form of the name in Primitive North West European speech was Tiwaz. That is to say, there were people in North West Europe who worshipped at the time of Christ a god called Tiwaz; and as a name and a personage Tiwaz was equivalent to Sanskrit Dyaus, Greek Zeus and Roman Jovis. The name Tiwaz gave rise to Ziu among the Germans, Tyr among the Scandinavians and Tiw among the English, and all these forms are recorded.

I base my claim for the identification of Tiwaz with the Sky Father on a number of arguments to be presently set forth, and first on the etymological connection of the names Tiwaz, Jovis, Zeus, Dyaus and Djevs. The eminent authorities Chadwick, Shetelig and Falk deny the connection between Tiwaz and Djevs, their contention being that *tiwaz* (with a small *t*) had come to mean simply 'god'. This may be so: the old word may have been used to mean 'god', but in any religion the use of the word 'god' alone is invariably a reference to the *chief* god, and so this argument appears to me to favour the identification of Tiwaz with Djevs rather than otherwise. But, in fact, there is no inherent improbability about the etymological relationship between Tiwaz, Jovis, Zeus, Dyaus and Djevs; and the Danish scholar Gudmund Schütte lends the weight of his authority to this contention in his monumental work *Our Forefathers*. In the light of ancillary evidence it becomes pedantic and even ridiculous to deny that Tiwaz was once Djevs the Sky Father.

Perhaps the most effective arguments to support the identification are those based on the use by the North West European tribes of Tiwaz in place-names and as a title for one of the days of the week. If we are to accept the evidence of place-names, all the North West European tribes had at one time believed Tiwaz to be extremely important. Take, for example, Zierberg in Bavaria; Diensberg and Zierenberg in Hesse; Tisdorf and Zeisberg in Saxe-Weimar; Tystathe and Tuslunde in Jutland; Tisvelae in Zealand; Tistad, Tisby, Tisjö and Tyved in Sweden; while in England we have Tuesley (Surrey), Tysoe (Warwickshire) and the lost Tislea (Hampshire), Tyesmere (Worcestershire) and Tifield (Sussex). In Norway there is a memory of the god in the island of Tysnes in south Hordaland. No places at all were named after him in Iceland.

This distribution of place-names containing the local form of Tiw indicates that he was an important god; secondly, it knocks on the head the contention that this was not a personal name but meant only 'god'; thirdly, it shows that he was important in what we now call Germany, south Denmark and Sweden, but to a lesser extent in Norway; and fourthly, that he was still worshipped by the English after AD 450, but that four hundred years later (AD 874) when Norwegians colonized Iceland, he no longer had devotees among them who desired to name settlements after him. However, since later records show Thor to have been very popular in Iceland (more popular than Odinn if the frequency of 'Thor' as an element in personal names and place-names is a guide); and since in the end Frey became chief god in Sweden, and Woden chief god in England, then we must believe that Tiwaz sank in the social scale and was no longer regarded by North West European tribes in later years as the Sky Father. This observation is borne out by Tiwaz' having given his name to the third day of the week. For among the present-day descendants of the North West European tribes that day (like our own Tuesday) is generally called after Tiwaz. This naming affords a clue to the new niche into which the god had been pushed. For although he was still remembered, he was no longer supreme; he was no longer regarded as the Sky Father and head of the pantheon, but had dwindled to a lesser god, a god of war and soldiers. We can tell that Tiwaz was gradually changed from a sky god to a war god at the beginning of the Christian era from a clue contained in our calendar. Sometime after AD 300 the North West Europeans accepted Roman names for their months along with the seven-day week translated into terms of their native deities; and Tuesday, Old English *Tiwes-dæg*, corresponds to the Latin *Martis dies*, the day of Mars, Roman god of war. And the fact that Tiw was regarded as a war god is well established by other evidence such as the seventh-century Kentish Epinal Gloss which translates Mars by Tiig, i.e. Tiw.

If the chief god is removed from his place a vacuum is created, and mythology abhors a vacuum as much as nature does: another god must move in. Actually, Woden moved in, but it will be more convenient to discuss this, as well as when the supersession took place, in the next chapter.

If Tiwaz is accepted as the old Sky Father one might go on to inquire if there are any myths still extant in which he figures *as* the Sky Father. I have to acknowledge at once that there is no *direct* reference to Tiwaz as a Sky Father among the literary remains of any of the North West European tribes. In other words, when we hear of Ziu, Tyr or Tiw he is always spoken of as god of war. Even the myths attached to Tiw's name as a war god have disappeared along with all the other myths from Old English records.

But it is possible by hypothesis and reference to Old Norse tales to uncover a number of myths which there is adequate reason to believe were originally told of the Sky Father: and that is what I now propose to do.

Because the Hindus, Greeks and Romans referred to a chief god sometimes called Dyauspitar, Zeuspater and Jupiter, we might have expected to find a North West European form of the chief god's name which also had the local word for 'father' fastened on the end. Such a form would have been *Tiwazfader*.

It is nowhere to be found.

But there is a memory in Norse myth of a god who was once the chief deity, who was there 'in the beginning' and who did have 'father' as part of his name, being called in fact Alföðr or Allfather. I am going to argue that Norse Allfather and Tiwaz were originally one and the same.

Most of the information about Allfather comes from one source, the mythically late *Prose Edda* written by Snorri Sturluson who died in 1241. Snorri identifies Odinn with Allfather, but it is clear that these two gods were never one; though it is obvious why Snorri makes the identification, namely because Odinn had usurped Tiwaz' place. In answer to the questions 'Who is the One who was there from the beginning of time? Who is the oldest of the gods?' Snorri answers:

> He is called Allfather (so they say) and in the Ancient Asgard he had twelve names: First Allfather, second Lord (or Lord of Armies), third Spear Lord, fourth Smiter, then All-knowing, Fulfiller-of-wishes, Farspoken, Shaker, Burner, Destroyer, Protector and twelfth Gelding. . . . He lives through all time and he rules his kingdom with absolute power over all things great and small. . . . He created heaven and earth and sky and everything within them . . . but most wonderful was when he created man and gave him spirit which shall be eternal and never fail though the body drop to dust or burn to ashes.

Here is confusion indeed, for Allfather is said to be 'the oldest of the gods', to have been there 'from the beginning of time', to have 'created heaven and earth and sky and all within them', to have 'created man', to be the ruler of his kingdom 'with absolute power'; and yet he shares some of these attributes with the god called Odinn. For Odinn (with his two brothers Vili and Vé), is also said to have created heaven, earth and man; and Odinn like Allfather, is called at one time or another by the twelve names used for Allfather. Indeed, in both the *Verse Edda* and the *Prose Edda* 'Allfather' is used as a synonym of 'Odinn'. But Odinn did *not* live from the beginning of time; he was not just *there*, but was born of the union of the god Bor and the giantess Bestla; nor did Odinn 'rule his kingdom with absolute power' – he was at the mercy of Fate: both Snorri and the ancient verses are agreed on these points. There can be no doubt but that Allfather and Odinn (no matter how they got mixed up later on) were originally two different personages.

Then who was Allfather? As we shall see, the myths connected with his name are those most applicable to a sky god, as indeed is Snorri's description of him in his Prologue to his *Edda* as:

> a governor of the stars of heaven: one who might order their courses after his will, very strong and full of might. People also held this to be true: that if he swayed the chief things of creation, he must have been before the stars of heaven; and they saw that if he ruled the courses of the heavenly bodies, he must also govern the shining of the sun, and the dews of the air, and the fruits of the earth, whatsoever grows upon it; and in like manner the winds of the air and the storms of the sea. They knew not yet where his kingdom was; but this they believed: that he ruled all things on earth and in the sky, the great stars also of the heavens and the winds of the sea.

Now, if Allfather was chief god, a sky god in particular, and in addition father of all, there can be little doubt that he was 'Tiwazfader' the old original Sky Father.

It then becomes a reasonable assumption that the myths in which Allfather figures in Norse sources, especially where they have obvious sky affinities, are myths which were once told of Tiwaz; and it is at least possible that our own Anglo-Saxon forefathers must have remembered some such tales which had once been told of Tiw.

Tiw, then, was originally the Creator: under his title Allfather he is depicted in the *Prose Edda* as the prime mover in one creation myth which goes as follows: once upon a time there was a giant called Nökkvi. He appears to be connected with the moon, for his name in other Indo-European languages turns up in various forms meaning 'ship'; and Nökkvi seems to be the helmsman of the moon regarded as a vessel sailing across the starry heavens. Nökkvi had a daughter called Night who was dark and dusky-haired, taking after her family (says Snorri). The maiden Night was given in marriage to three suitors called Naglfar, Annarr and Delling. These names mean Twilight, the 'Second' and Dawn. Night had a child by each of these fathers: by Twilight she had a son named Space, by the 'Second' a daughter named Earth, and by Dawn another son who took after his father's side, being bright and fair; he was called Day. All the personages in this story are of the sky; but where is the Sky Father?

The clue to solve the mystery lies with Annarr, the 'Second'. In his *Edda* Snorri identifies Annarr with Odinn and says that Earth was his daughter and his wife also. Here is a case of attributes being transferred from one god to another, for when Odinn became chief god he assumed the mantle of the one he had dispossessed: we can be fairly certain that the 'Second' was originally the Sky Father, that is to say Tiwaz or Tiw, and that Twilight, the 'Second' and Dawn are but three different manifestations of the one god, the ancient Djevs.

More than a suspicion that the ancient Anglo-Saxons recollected the myth of Annarr's (that is, the old Sky Father's or Tiw's) marriage to Earth is contained in the Old English *Charm* already quoted to restore fertility to the land:

Erce, Erce, Erce,	Erce, Erce, Erce,
eorthan modor,	Mother of Earth. . . .
hæl wes thu folde,	Hail to thee, Earth
fira modor!	Mother of men!
beo thu growende	grow and bring forth
on Godes fæthme.	in God's embrace.

This is no Christian or even Old Testament tale: divinity was never immanent in nature but transcended nature as far as the Jews were concerned: this is a pagan story of the wedding between the Sky Father and the Earth Mother.

When we return to the Icelandic sources we learn that Allfather or Tiw as the English knew him took Night and her son Day and giving each of them a pair of horses and a chariot, dispatched them up the heavens to drive round the earth once in every twenty-four hours. Night drove first with the horse known as Frostymane, who every morning sprinkles the grass with his dew which is really foam flying off as he champs his bit. Day's horse, Shiningmane, illumines all the earth and sky with the light from his hair.

There is a variant of this tale preserved side by side with it by the Icelandic writer. It tells of a being named Mundilfari who had two children so bright and fair that he had the temerity to call the boy Moon and the girl Sun. But the 'gods' paid Mundilfari out for his pride by snatching away the brother and sister and setting them to work in the heavens. They made Moon drive round with the moon while Sun became postilion to the horses pulling the chariot of the sun: these two horses are called Earlywake and Supreme-in-strength.

The roots of the chariot of the sun myth lie deep in Indo-European soil, for we see the flowers not only in northern story but in Greek, Roman and Hindu mythology as well. There is written provenance of the northern version going back to AD 98 in Tacitus' *Germania* 45:

> Passing the [tribe called] Suiones we find yet another sea [the Baltic] . . . believed to be the boundary that girdles the earth. . . . The last radiance of the setting sun lingers here until dawn with a brightness that makes the stars turn pale. There is a rumour that you can hear the sound he makes as he rises from the waves and can see the shape of his horses and the rays on his head.

44 Even further back in time, the sun-chariot idea is graphically represented in the Bronze Age sun image found at Trundholm.

Such myths as I have just traced from Icelandic sources were being put into verse round about AD 850–950, that is to say, some two or three hundred years after the conversion of the English. Changes in the original tales were only to be expected as the culture of the northern branch of the North West European peoples became diversified from the western branch and as their poets worked over the material. For one thing, the Northmen set out on a sustained venture of colonization by force which resulted in their settling half of England, parts of Scotland and Ireland, and Normandy. Because they had to fight their way into each of these regions they were apt to extol the military virtues and their chief god was looked upon as the final arbiter of battles. This chief god was no longer Tiwaz, but he assimilated most of Tiwaz' qualities and many of the myths (such as the sun myths just mentioned), formerly told of Tiwaz.

The Northmen did, however, retain one myth of the heavens which must always have been associated with Tiwaz' name. It appears that the Sun and Moon are galloping across the heavens because they are pursued by two wolves. The one chasing Sun is called Skoll; it is he who frightens her into flight and in the end he will capture her. The other wolf, leaping along behind Moon, is called Hati who intends to overtake Moon,

44 Bronze Age sun-chariot found at Trundholm, Denmark. The horse (there may originally have been a pair) is of bronze and the disc is gold-plated on one side. The connection is apparent between the image and the Indo-European myths – whether Greek, Roman or North West European – in which the sun is drawn round the heavens by horse and chariot.

and there can be no doubt but that he will succeed; for the account says:

> there lived a witch in the forest called Ironwood to the east of Midgard. In that same forest dwelt trollwives or Ironwooders. The ancient witch farrowed giants by the dozen and all in the likeness of wolves: it is from them that these two wolves come. Further, it is said, a really frightful one in line of descent called Moonhound shall throw out. He shall be filled with the flesh of all men who die; he shall swallow the Moon; and he shall sprinkle with blood all the sky and heavens at which the Sun's light shall be put out and winds shall rise up and howl hither and yon.

While the bones of this story are ancient North West European and without doubt Indo-European, the Northmen clothed them with a flesh of their own devising. They have given the myth a new shape which allows it to fall into place as a piece in their jigsaw puzzle which at last turns into a picture of the final destruction of heaven, earth, gods and men. This appears to be a peculiarly northern conception, probably to be narrowed down as only a Norwegian and Icelandic conception. There is no conclusive evidence that the Old English ever believed in the Ragnarök, the Doom of the Divine Powers: and yet there is a suspicion that they had heard of it and remembered it even after four hundred years of Christianity, when we find Wulfstan, Archbishop of York, crying out to the English in 1014:

This world is rushing on to its end: and the longer things have contact with the world the worse they become, as [because of people's sins] it must daily happen that evil will increase until the coming of Antichrist! Then indeed it will be horrible and terrifying throughout the world.

Was Wulfstan recalling Christian superstition, old native pagan traditions, or was he influenced by contemporary Viking beliefs? It is perhaps impossible to decide. One doubts whether the Anglo-Saxons ever developed a full-blown Ragnarök myth, but (as I hope to show later) there is evidence to indicate that they knew of the sun's being swallowed by a wolf and of the efforts made by the Sky Father, Tiw, to prevent this despoiling of his realm.

They may also have known the story of how the wolf Fenrir was shackled, which goes like this: the Æsir enticed Fenrir across a lake of the Underworld to an island where they made the last of three attempts to fetter him. Their first two bonds he had snapped easily. The third was different: it had been fashioned of most unusual materials by a dwarf in the land of the Dark Elves. The six ingredients forged into this fetter called Gleipnir were the noise of a cat's footfall, a woman's beard, the roots of a mountain, the nerves of a bear, a fish's breath and the spittle of a bird. When the wolf Fenrir saw the new shackle (which was smooth and soft as silk), he suspected sorcery and refused to be bound with it until a god had laid his hand between the wolf's jaws as a token of good faith. None wished to do this but at last Tyr offered his right fist, the fetter was fastened round the wolf's leg and no matter how Fenrir struggled, the bond cut the tighter, and he was unable to break loose. He bit off Tyr's hand.

The gods chained him to a lofty crag called Howling, and, lifting up an enormous boulder, they pile-drove the crag still deeper into the ground, using the boulder afterwards to weight down the crag. The wolf gaped terrifically, struggled madly and tried to bite; so they wedged a sword between his chops, the pommel at his bottom jaw and the point transfixing his palate: that gagged him somewhat. He bellowed hideously and bloody slaver roped down from his gob forming a river which the Northmen called Van. And there (they go on to say) he lies till the Ragnarök.

There are features in this story which have been worked up by the poets, for instance the ingredients of the fetter, the sword between the jaws and especially the northern idea of the wolf lying bound only until the Doom of the Divine Powers. Nevertheless, the basic story of a clash between the Sky Father and a monster who is cast down into the darkness goes back to the earliest Indo-European times, which is one reason for supposing that the Old English remembered it in some form similarly associated with Tiw. There are echoes of the gagging of Fenriswulf in a curious bit of history quoted by Lady Stenton in her *English Society in the Early Middle Ages*. She tells of a large company of people (thirteen are named) who hunted all day in Rockingham Forest in the year 1255 and who 'cut off the head of a buck and put it on a stake in the middle of a certain clearing . . . placing in the mouth of the afore-

45 Samson killing the lion, a fifteenth-century picture from Denmark. A literal
rendering of Judges xiv. 5–6, goes 'he tore the lion in pieces'. The artist translates
this as a tearing apart of the creature's jaws, a reminiscence possibly of the old pagan
myths of how the god Odinn was rescued from the belly of the wolf.

said head a certain spindle, and they made the mouth gape towards the sun in great contempt of the lord King and his foresters'.

Lady Stenton takes this behaviour to indicate that the hunters were 'certainly light hearted in their sport'. But there is surely something much deeper and (perhaps) darker than that. It is evident that here was some kind of ritual which was not really intended to mock the King and his verderers: the antlered head of the buck takes us back to the Palaeolithic cave-paintings and forward to the Abbots Bromley horn dance; the number of named hunters (thirteen) is that of the witch's coven as well as a commonly accepted number of the Old Norse gods; the making of the mouth gape towards the sun is surely significant.

Is it too much to claim that here was a fundamentally magico-religious ceremony which our ancestors retained in their folklore from prehistoric times and which we occasionally glimpse in history books as well as in myths like that of Fenriswulf? In actual fact, the Rockingham poachers of 1255 were perpetuating a prehistoric ritual which was similar to that practised up to recent times by the Hairy Ainu of Japan when they appeased the spirit of the bear they had hunted to death by setting up his head on a pole.

There is another version of the clash in the account of how the Northmen's Odinn (again at the Ragnarök) was swallowed by the wolf. The northern poets suppressed the real ending to *that* story: in order for it to fit into their conception of the destruction of everything, Odinn was deemed to have died in the encounter. A mention is made of how Odinn's son Vidarr revenges himself upon the wolf by stepping with one foot into the animal's bottom jaw while with his arms he prises and tears the great gob apart. A killing of this nature could have only one end in view, that is to allow the swallowed god to emerge unscathed.

At the Ragnarök, Tyr himself is said to meet his end in an encounter with the hound from hell called Garm. This is but another version of the swallowing myth, with Tyr playing his (that is, Tiwaz') original part.

One last story of the Sky Father is mentioned rather cryptically by Snorri Sturluson in his *Prose Edda*: speaking of a mysterious being called Mimir, he relates how one of the three roots of the World Ash Tree twists in the direction of the Frost Giants who live beyond the ocean encircling the world. Under this root is Mimir's well, called after its guardian Mimir. 'The Allfather', says Snorri, 'came there looking for a draught from the well, but he didn't get it until he had put one of his eyes in pawn.' Directly connected with this is the northern depiction of Odinn as one-eyed. But it was not really Odinn who lost an eye, it was the old Sky Father. In these recollections is to be discerned the mythical explanation of the sun's nightly disappearance from the heavens, for the eye of the Sky Father is an emblem of the sun, while Mimir's well is a representation of the ocean. In like manner, the swallowing of the sky god by a monster invariably from the Underworld of darkness can be only a mythopoeic way of showing the *temporary* disappearance from the heavens of the supreme deity each time the sun sets: likewise, the deity comes forth fresh and new from the monster's jaws every sunrise.

45

46 Aerial view of the Royal Cemetery at Sutton Hoo overlooking the River Deben. Only one mound lies open at the re-excavation twenty years after its first discovery; from this mound (raised perhaps in honour of King Redwald) was taken the fabulous ship treasure now in the British Museum.

It may be objected that this myth is all very well for the Northmen but that there is no shred of direct evidence for its ever having been current among the English in England. Fortunately for my theory, I believe that there *is* evidence: only recently was it brought to light after the manner of the Sky Father himself out of twelve hundred years of darkness. In 1939 a mound at Sutton Hoo, one of a number on the east   46
bank of the River Deben in Suffolk, was excavated and found to contain the shadow of a ship. I say 'shadow' because the timber strakes had long   47
since mouldered to dust, though their lines were visible in the sandy soil, as were the rusty stains of the clench-nails. The buried vessel had been a

47, 48 'A shadow of a ship': the timbers had rotted and the iron clench nails rusted away, but on excavation the impression of the Sutton Hoo ship was still visible even after nearly thirteen hundred years. *Below*, Stuart Piggott's drawing showing the position of the finds at the time of the dig, 1939.

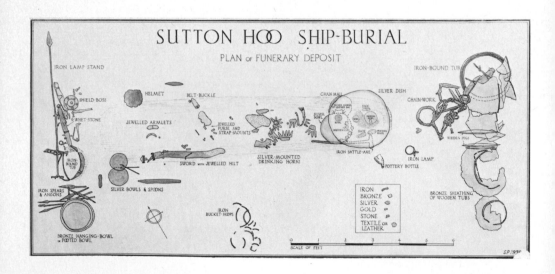

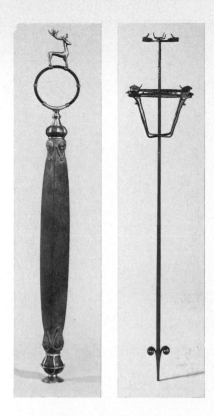

49, 50 Two recently reconstructed ceremonial objects from the Sutton Hoo ship: *right* a whetstone with carved heads and surmounted by a stag; *far right* a king's standard which recalls the golden one set up at Scyld Scefing's head when his corpse was given 'to the ocean, letting the waves roll him away'.

large rowing-boat unfit for further service, eighty feet long, fourteen feet in beam and drawing two feet of water. It had accommodation for more than thirty rowers. The undertakers had erected a little house of oak boards amidships in which was found buried treasure indeed. There were thirteen pieces of Byzantine silverware, nine silver-mounted drinking-horns and a number of small gourds mounted with gold; there was a silver-coloured iron helmet of ornate design with a face-shaped visor and a similarly ornate shield; there was a set of buckles, clasps and other fittings in gold richly decorated with cloisonné-work of garnet, mosaic glass and filigree; there was also a standard of wrought iron; and, in addition to this and other objects, there were a sword and a rich purse-top embellished with seven cloisonné plaques. Nor was the purse empty: it held a heap of thirty-seven Merovingian gold coins which made it sure that the date of their hoarding was no later than AD 630. All this treasure had been placed in the earth to honour some East Anglian warrior of high rank, perhaps a king, possibly Æthelhere father of that Aldwulf who remembered as a boy seeing King Redwald's pagan shrine. No trace of any body was found, so it seems that the ship and its furniture under the mound were intended to be a memorial or cenotaph to a leader who had perished at sea or in distant parts. Æthelhere himself died or was drowned at the Battle of Winwaed in Yorkshire on 15 November 655. But it may still be, as was first thought, that the ship burial was to honour King Redwald who died in AD 625 or 626.

48
57
51–53
43
50
43
54

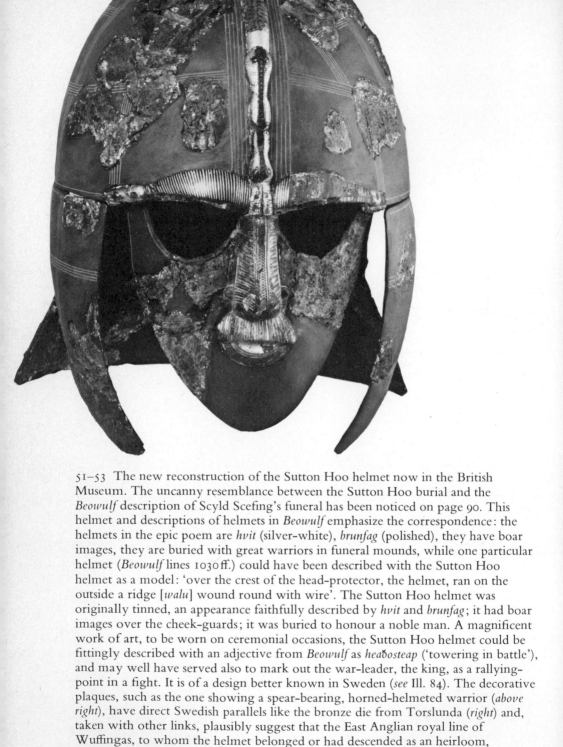

51–53 The new reconstruction of the Sutton Hoo helmet now in the British Museum. The uncanny resemblance between the Sutton Hoo burial and the *Beowulf* description of Scyld Scefing's funeral has been noticed on page 90. This helmet and descriptions of helmets in *Beowulf* emphasize the correspondence: the helmets in the epic poem are *hvit* (silver-white), *brunfag* (polished), they have boar images, they are buried with great warriors in funeral mounds, while one particular helmet (*Beowulf* lines 1030 ff.) could have been described with the Sutton Hoo helmet as a model: 'over the crest of the head-protector, the helmet, ran on the outside a ridge [*walu*] wound round with wire'. The Sutton Hoo helmet was originally tinned, an appearance faithfully described by *hvit* and *brunfag*; it had boar images over the cheek-guards; it was buried to honour a noble man. A magnificent work of art, to be worn on ceremonial occasions, the Sutton Hoo helmet could be fittingly described with an adjective from *Beowulf* as *heaðosteap* ('towering in battle'), and may well have served also to mark out the war-leader, the king, as a rallying-point in a fight. It is of a design better known in Sweden (*see* Ill. 84). The decorative plaques, such as the one showing a spear-bearing, horned-helmeted warrior (*above right*), have direct Swedish parallels like the bronze die from Torslunda (*right*) and, taken with other links, plausibly suggest that the East Anglian royal line of Wuffingas, to whom the helmet belonged or had descended as an heirloom, originated in Sweden.

54 A collection of Merovingian gold coins and two small ingots found with the Sutton Hoo purse.

43   It is the Sutton Hoo purse-top which, for the moment, is of importance
to us: for a pair of the ornamental plaques on it represent a figure in
55   human form about to be swallowed by two animals. Both person and
animals are stylized, but to my mind there can be little doubt that the
animal is intended to represent a wolf (duplicated for symmetry), while
the figure has a head of broken outline most like a child's drawing of the
sun. Admitted, the British Museum Provisional Guide says doubtfully
that the design may be a version of the 'Daniel in the Lions' Den' motif
familiar from Frankish buckles. But in those designs the lions are usually
fawning at Daniel's feet. The Sutton Hoo design is much more like a
56   similar Scandinavian one on a stamp for embossing bronze helmet-
plates from Torslunda, Sweden. In both the Torslunda and Sutton Hoo
designs the animals have gaping jaws attempting to swallow the figure's
head. I have little doubt in my own mind that the Sutton Hoo design,
the Torslunda stamp and the Frankish 'Daniel in the Lions' Den' motif
are all descended from one archetype and that the archetype is to be
found in Crete. It is the tableau depicting the 'Goddess of Animals', and
90, 91   also the 'Master of Animals' which is found there. Just as heads or animal
designs on ancient coinage change at first imperceptibly, but at last to
such an extent that what was originally a horse becomes a mere meaningless squiggle, so generations of craftsmen in different environments
changed the 'Goddess of Animals' to 'Daniel in the Lions' Den' or to the
Sky Father being swallowed by wolves. It is the culture within which the
craftsman worked which has finally shaped his design. I am convinced
that here on the Sutton Hoo purse-mount, in East Anglian craftsmanship
of some time before AD 650, is a memory of the Sky Father being
swallowed by the Wolf.

55, 56 Wolves swallowing the old Sky Father. This motif is found twice on the Sutton Hoo purse-top (*see* Ill. 43) and may be compared with the bronze die from Torslunda, Sweden (*below*).

57 Byzantine silver plate found in the Sutton Hoo ship. No one can say for certain how this 'decorated treasure from a far-off land' found its way from what the Vikings were later to call Micklegarth, the Great City of the World, to the banks of the tiny English River Deben.

There is more to the Sutton Hoo ship-burial than this, for in addition to this exciting link with the Sky Father, there is another, no less exciting, with that pagan hero already mentioned in some detail, namely Scyld Scefing.

We saw how Scyld Scefing drifted to Scania in an open boat; when at last he died, his people, according to *Beowulf* (lines 26–52) gave him a rich ship-burial:

When his time came, the old warrior Scyld passed away from them into the Lord's protection. Then his own dear comrades bore him to the edge of the sea, just as he had asked them to. They had taken heed of his words during his time as protector of the Scyldings. The chieftain's ship, icy and eager to set sail, lay with its ring-carved stern drawn up on the hard: they carried this famous and generous prince to a last resting-place by the mast in the bosom of the boat. To that spot they brought decorated treasures from far-off lands: never did I hear of a more splendid vessel in its adornment of war weapons, battle-coats, swords and corselets. Many precious things lay about his body that were to pass with him into the power of the sea. They girded his corse with no less gifts, with the heirlooms of a people, than they had done who had set him adrift in the beginning, alone as a little child. In addition, they affixed high at his head a golden standard: then they gave him to the ocean, letting the waves roll him away. Sad were their hearts, mournful their minds. No one, no counsellor in the hall, could tell for certain, ever, who received that burden.

The resemblances between this description and what was found at Sutton Hoo are so striking as to be uncanny. It is almost as if the *Beowulf* poet was giving an eyewitness account of what was being placed in that East Anglian ship at the very period he was writing. There are important differences, of course; the Sutton Hoo ship was buried not cast adrift, nor were there signs of a body; but there is quite a long list of similarities. Both have richly ornamented treasures cached amidships; both have treasures brought from afar – from Byzantium in the case of the Sutton Hoo ship; both have various weapons, swords and corselets; and both have a prince's standard.

57

This is not the place to inquire into the general meaning of ship-burial: we may note for the moment that it was a custom of our princely pagan ancestors mentioned by poets and substantiated by finds. In the objects brought to light at Sutton Hoo we are fortunate to have corroboration of some of our theories concerning the myths and gods of the Old English, including the swallowing of the Sky Father. From that nightly swallowing the sky god returned each morning: after his later deposition by the Northmen he was not allowed to return.

It is now time to ask about the god who usurped the Sky Father's place among the North West European peoples, a god who was at one period admitted to be supreme by many of the Old English. His name to them was Woden.

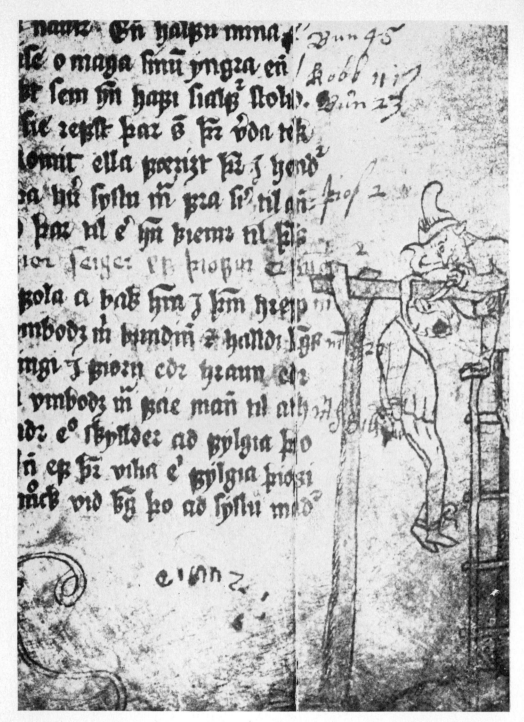

58 One of Odinn's nicknames was Gallows God. This drawing comes from a sixteenth-century source, the Arnamagnean Collection, Copenhagen.

If a West Saxon farmer in pagan times had walked out of his *bury* or *ton* above the Vale of Pewsey some autumn day, and looking up to the hills *32* had caught sight of a bearded stranger seeming in long cloak larger than life as he stalked the skyline through low cloud; and if they had met at the gallows by the cross-roads where a body still dangled; and if the *58* farmer had noticed the old wanderer glancing up from under a shadowy hood or floppy brimmed hat with a gleam of recognition out of his one piercing eye as though acclaiming a more than ordinary interest, a possessive interest, in the corpse; and if a pair of ravens had tumbled out of the mist at that moment, and a couple of wolves howled one to the other in some near-by wood; and if the stranger had been helping himself along with a massive spear larger by far than normal; and if all this had induced in the beholder a feeling of awe; then he would have been justified in believing that he was in the presence of Woden tramping the world of men over his own Wansdyke. *30*

Such a picture may appear, these days, fanciful. But there is evidence to suggest it all in our own native English sources. We know from place-names that there was a centre of Woden worship above the Vale of Pewsey; in fact, if place-names are any guide, Woden was the most widely honoured of the heathen gods in England, for we find him commemorated as the patron of settlements among the Angles of Northumbria, the East and West Saxons of Essex and Wessex, and the Jutes of Kent. There is no shadow of a doubt that the aristocracy of the Old English looked upon Woden as chief god: the genealogies of the kings bear witness to the former dignity of Woden's name, for even in Christian times the royal houses of Kent, Essex, Wessex, Deira, Bernicia and East Anglia all traced back to Woden.

But who *was* Woden if Tiw had originally been the old Sky Father and chief of the gods? In order to answer this question we may first confine ourselves to native evidence and begin with the name 'Woden'. The Primitive West Europeans had all called him Wodenaz, a name which developed into Wuotan in Old High German, into Wodan in Old Saxon, into Voden (later Odinn) in Old Norse, and into Woden in Old English. We can therefore accept him as a Primitive West European god known to all the tribes of the group.

There is a dispute, still unsettled, as to what were the antecedents and relatives of the word Wodenaz in Indo-European languages. There are two possible explanations. One suggests that Wodenaz was first believed to be a wind or storm god with power over the dead; and the other that he was a divine magician who by self-sacrifice had brought wisdom to men. There is evidence that the Old English believed Woden to possess attributes which reflect both characters: in short, he was for them both a god of wisdom and a god of the dead.

We may examine the two sides of Woden's character in turn, and first that suggested by those who derive the name Wodenaz from an Indo-European word which is also the parent of Sanskrit *vata* and Latin *ventus* meaning 'wind'. Wodenaz would then be a god of wind and storm like the Hindu Vata, lord of the wind. In his turn, Woden is taken to be a deified development of the German storm giant Wode leading his 'wild army' (*das wütende Heer*), his procession of the homeless dead across the sky. This view is supported by Adam of Bremen's definition 'Wodan, that is to say Fury' (*Wodan, id est furor*), and by the Anglo-Saxon *wodendream* which is glossed into Latin as *furor animi*, and also by the fact that in Sweden *das wütende Heer* is known as *Odens jagt* or 'Woden's Hunt'. This is the Odinn who in Old Norse sources is identified with the eight-legged stallion Sleipnir. Some authorities would have it that Wodenaz and his steed were originally identical and that if the rider of the eight-legged horse depicted on the gravestone at Tjängride in Gothland represents a dead man being carried away by the horse-demon and not Odinn mounted on Sleipnir, then this conception was still current in Gothland in much later times.

There is excellent evidence for this side of Woden's character in Old English sources. The belief in Woden's Hunt lived long and vividly in native story and folklore: it still continues to do so in the superstition (suitably revamped by Christians) of Gabriel's Hounds; while as recently as 1939 the myth has reappeared in a popular American cowboy song, the 'Riders in the Sky', in which the homeless dead are a ghostly 'devil's herd' of cattle whose 'brands wuz still on fire' and whose 'hooves wuz made of steel', while Woden is represented as a ghostly cowboy condemned to a terrible eternity of rounding-up 'across these endless skies'. But the version of the Wild Hunt which is closest to that imagined by the pagan Old English is to be found in the *Anglo-Saxon Chronicle* under the entry for AD 1127:

> Let no one be surprised at what we are about to relate, for it was common gossip up and down the countryside that after February 6th many people both saw and heard a whole pack of huntsmen in full cry. They straddled black horses and black bucks while their hounds were pitch black with staring hideous eyes. This was seen in the very deer park of Peterborough town, and in all the woods stretching from that same spot as far as Stamford. All through the night monks heard them sounding and winding their horns. Reliable witnesses who kept watch in the night declared that there might well have been twenty or even thirty of them in this wild tantivy as near as they could tell.

59

59 Gravestone from Tjängride, Gothland showing Odinn's eight-legged stallion
Sleipnir with a rider who may be Odinn himself, or possibly the god Hermod on
his way to Hel to find Balder (*see* Ill. 87).

One might object that there is no mention of Woden here; but we can be quite sure that the Old English did regard Woden as a leader of a wild hunt of the lost souls or homeless dead because of their identifying him with the Roman god Mercury, the *psychopompos* or 'leader of souls' of Classical myth. We find this identification of Woden with Mercury as well as Woden's patronage of the dead in a tenth-century alliterative homily printed in Kemble's *Solomon and Saturn*:

Sum man was gehaten	Once there lived a man
Mercurius on life;	who was Mercury called;
he was swithe facenful	he was vastly deceitful
and swicol on dedum	and cunning in his deeds,
and lufode eac stala	he loved well to steal
and leasbrednysse;	and all lying tricks;
thone macodon tha hæthenan	the heathens had made him
him to mæran gode	the highest of their gods,
and æt wega galaetum	and at the cross-roads
him lac offrodon	they offered him booty
and to heagum beorgum	and to the high hills
him on brohton onsegdnysse.	brought him victims to slay.
Thes god was awurthra	This god was most honoured
betwux eallum hæthenum	among all the heathen;
and he is Othon gehaten	his name when translated
othrum namen on Denisc.	to Danish is Odinn.

This identification of Woden with Mercury is borne out by the name we still use for the fourth day of the week. The Romans came to call that day after Mercury, namely *Mercurii dies*, which we still find in modern French as *mercredi*. When our ancestors adopted the Roman calendar they called the fourth day after their god whom they supposed corresponded to Mercury: and that was Woden, hence *Wodnes-dæg*, modern Wednesday. Woden and Mercury were identified because of their connection with the leading of the souls of the dead; and we can be certain of this, because if Woden had been identified with the *chief* god of the Romans then his name would have been given to the fifth day of the week 'Jove's day' which has become *jeudi* in French.

Perhaps I may now deal with the other main characteristic of the god of the dead, his magical wisdom. This is implicit in his name, say the authorities who do not hold with the etymology of Wodenaz which I have already discussed, but who declare that the name is related to Latin *vates* and Irish *faith*, a sort of bard. Among the Gauls the *vates* was more of a wizard, a combination of soothsayer and sacrificial priest as we gather from Strabo who says 'the bards are minstrels and poets, but the *vates* are offerers of sacrifices and interpreters of nature.' We may note in passing that Saxo Grammaticus calls Odinn *vates*.

Once again there is native evidence for this side of Woden's character; our English forebears have left clues which prove they were well aware of Woden's skill as a wizard or sorcerer or *vates* in one of the oldest pieces of extant Anglo-Saxon verse, the *Nine Herbs Charm*:

The snake came crawling and struck at none. But Woden took nine glory-twigs and struck the adder so that it flew into nine parts. . . .

The word usually translated 'glory-twigs', that is *wuldortanas*, is itself interesting, for the first element is the local form in England of Primitive West European *Wolthuthliwaz* found on a sword-scabbard from Denmark dating to about AD 300 and in later (*c.* AD 800) Norse myth as Ullr. Ullr is an obscure god, but his name appears to have meant 'splendour', which, together with his other attributes tends to identify him with the Sky Father. So the *wuldortanas* may be reasonably taken to represent the 'twigs of Wuldor' or of the Sky Father. At any rate, we know that in actual fact the *wuldortanas* were twigs on which runic signs had been cut. This takes us back to Tacitus, who, writing in AD 98, mentions (in *Germania* 10) that our Western European ancestors had the highest possible regard for auspices and the casting of lots. He goes on:

> their procedure in casting lots is uniform. They break off the branch of a fruit tree and slit it into strips; they mark these with different runes and cast them at random on to a white cloth. Then, according to whether the consultation is a public or private one, the priest of the state or father of the family, after a prayer to the gods and an intent gaze heavenwards, picks up three, one at a time, and reads their meaning from the runes scored on them.

The problem of the origin of runes and their earliest use seems now to be more or less settled. According to the latest authorities, our ancestors received the runic alphabet through northern Italy, and their first development of it was not for writing or reading but magically for divination. And the god most closely connected with these symbols was Wodenaz: we may be sure of this from the Old English evidence of the *Nine Herbs Charm* quoted above, where the 'glory-twigs' are slivers of wood with runes cut into them, and from Old Norse evidence which makes Odinn the discoverer of runes. Wodenaz was taken to be the wise magician; nor is this a later and one-sided development of Woden by the Old English or of Odinn by the Northmen.

The association of Woden-Odinn with runes and wisdom is reflected in two passages of Old English and Old Norse verse which have occasioned a good deal of debate. There is, however, no possibility of doubt about their real meaning which is the same in either case: that the god by self-sacrifice won knowledge for the benefit of men. The Old English reference is again from the *Nine Herbs Charm*:

> Thyme and fennel, a pair great in power,
> the wise Lord, holy in heaven,
> wrought these herbs while he hung on the cross;
> he placed them and put them in the seven worlds
> to aid all, rich and poor.

While in the Norse passage Odinn himself tells of his wild experience in stanzas 138, 139 and 141 of the *Lay of the High One*:

I trow that I hung
on the windy tree,
    swung there nights all of nine;
gashed with a blade
bloodied for Odinn,
    myself an offering to myself
knotted to that tree
no man knows
    whither the roots of it runs.

None gave me bread
none gave me drink,
    down to the depths I peered
to snatch up runes
with a roaring screech
    and fall in a dizzied faint!

Wellbeing I won
and wisdom too,
    I grew and joyed in my growth;
from a word to a word
I was led to a word
    from a deed to another deed.

Whether this conception of the god's self-immolation on the cross in one case or the 'windy tree' (Yggdrasill) in the other grew out of, or was modified by the Christian account of Calvary is perhaps an insoluble problem. But we can be quite certain that the Old English did regard Woden as a god of wisdom: not only is there the conclusive evidence of the *Nine Herbs Charm*, but there is also the verse homily quoted. There, in order to discredit the god and make him a devil, the Christian homilist has turned Woden's original attributes upside down, so that wisdom becomes deceit and slyness. But he has recorded, too, Woden's link with hanging, for thus were victims offered to the god 'at the crossroads'.

Old Norse sources give a very full account of Odinn: the problem is to know how far the Old English conception of Woden is paralleled in the comparatively late Norse traditions of the tenth century concerning Odinn, lord of Valhalla.

The poems of the *Verse Edda* yield the following information: warriors killed honourably on the battlefield find their way to Odinn in his hall of the slain Valhöll, anglicized as Valhalla. This edifice, shining bright with gold, is easily recognized for its rafters are spears, it is tiled with shields, the benches are strewn with war-coats, and over the western door hangs a wolf with an eagle hovering above it. Here every day does Odinn 'choose men killed with weapons'. There are 550 doors in Valhalla's walls, each wide enough to allow through eight hundred men marching abreast, shoulder to shoulder, at one time. These doors are mentioned as being for use particularly when the warriors double forth to 'fight with the Wolf', that is to say at the time of the Ragnarök. But the outermost entry port called Valgrind, 'the holy

60 Sketch from the Utrecht Psalter of a battle scene typical of what the Norsemen imagined to take place daily in Valhalla.

barred-gate of the slain' of which 'few people can tell how tightly it is locked', is the one door to Valhalla which those newly killed in battle must enter. Even before they reach Valgrind, the 'host of the slain' must wade through the loudly roaring Thund, the river of air. Once safely past these obstacles, 'the men killed with weapons' enter Valhalla: here they indulge the two hugest appetites of the Viking, feasting and fighting. Their meat is prepared in a mighty cauldron holding enough succulent stew to feed them all; and its main ingredient is the flesh of a magical boar who, though stuck and dressed for table one day, is nevertheless alive and ready for the same treatment the next. The warriors' tipple is the sparkling mead which spirts from the teats of the nanny goat Heidrun who browses on the branches of Lærad the tree standing outside Valhalla.

According to Snorri Sturluson writing two hundred years after the composition of the poems of the *Verse Edda* (from which the above account is drawn) the Chosen Warriors or Einheriar:

> every day as soon as they are dressed don their armour, file orderly on to the parade ground, fight and flatten each other: that is their sport; then, when second breakfast time comes they scamper home to Valhalla and sit themselves down to their drinking . . .

60

This is a sophisticated account, but the idea of an 'everlasting battle' is probably old and may be mythological; Snorri quotes a stanza from a *Verse Edda* poem to show that he is not fabricating the story himself:

> All the Einheriar
> in Odinn's barracks
>   crack each other's crowns every day;
> they bundle up the dead
> ride back from the fight . . .
>   and down sit to drink all healed.

This stanza comes from the *Lay of Vafthrudnir* and is the only *Verse Edda* poem to mention the 'everlasting battle'. But the 'everlasting battle' is a common theme not only in Norse story but in Celtic tales too; yet nowhere in the earliest sources (except in the stanza quoted above) is it connected with the Chosen Warriors in Valhalla. It is not even mentioned – and this is significant – in the fullest of the verse sources describing Valhalla and the Einheriar, namely the *Lay of Grimnir*; so I conclude that originally the idea of the 'everlasting battle' existed separately from that of the Chosen Slain. The two came together in a larger process of agglutination which in the end resulted in the awe-inspiring conception of the Doom of the Gods, the Ragnarök. We thus see the myth as a living entity growing and altering even on Norse soil: how much alteration took place after the Western and Northern European peoples had separated is not so easy to decide.

Further information from Snorri is that 'Odinn is called Valfather or Father of the Slain because all those who fall in battle are his sons by adoption; he billets them in Valhalla and Vingolf and they are called Einheriar or Champions.' He says, too, of the goddess Freya that 'she rides to battle and takes one half of the corpses and Odinn the other half', quoting the *Lay of Grimnir* to support him:

> Half of the dead
> Freya chooses each day
>   and Odinn rakes up the rest.

Associated with Odinn as a god of the dead are the Valkyries. Says Snorri, 'their lot is to wait on in Valhalla, to carry round the drinks, to keep the table going and the ale-cups brimming. . . . Odinn despatches them to every battle where they make a choice of men destined to die, and decide who shall have victory.' The word *valkyrja* means a 'female chooser of the slain'; there is, too, a phrase in Old Norse *kjose val*, 'to choose the slain', whose real meaning (simple as it seems) is uncertain. The phrase may mean either to pick up the dead from the battlefield, or to decide upon those who are to die on the battlefield. In general, both the *Prose* and *Verse Eddas'* picture of the Valkyries is of a domesticated type of warrior woman who is equally at home serving drink in the hall or riding splendidly horsed and armed above the battlefield. Such is the picture of them in the *Lay of Helgi the Slayer of Hunding*:

High under helmets
across the field of heaven,
> their breastplates all
> were blotched with blood,
and from their spear points
sparks flashed forth.

But there is a memory of something wilder, fiercer, much more primitive and unconventional in such eddaic Valkyrie names as *Hlökk* (Shrieker), *Göll* (Screamer) and *Skögul* (Raging). This memory of cruder figures is even stronger in the skaldic poem, the *Lay of Darts*; here the Valkyries weave the web of war much as Gray depicted them in his version of the poem which he called the *Fatal Sisters*. The *Lay of Darts* is spoken by Valkyries who call themselves Odinn's friends and who tell of a great warp raised on spears into which they are running a red weft. This web of victory (and here we recall *Beowulf*) is dripping with blood; the warp itself is made of men's guts weighted at the bottom with human heads; the shuttles are arrows; and the Valkyries say plainly that they are able to order victory or defeat in battle, after which they cry 'Let us ride off far away on our bare-backed steeds with our drawn swords in our hands!'

Such creatures, exulting in blood and slaughter, are unlike the dignified Amazons of Snorri; but they are akin to those others mentioned in the sagas, creatures for instance such as those dreamed of by King Harald Hardradi's men before their ill-fated expedition left Norway to fight Harold of England in 1066 at Stamford Bridge. On this occasion, one man Gyrth 'had a dream in which he thought he was on the king's ship when he saw a great witch-wife standing on the island, with a fork in one hand and a trough in the other . . .'. Evidently the fork was intended to rake up the dead and the trough to catch the blood. Another man, Tord, dreamt that 'before the army of the people of the country was riding a huge witch-wife upon a wolf; and the wolf had a man's carcass in his mouth, and the blood dripping from his jaws; and when he had eaten up one body she threw another into his mouth, and so one after another, and he swallowed them all'.

In the past two hundred years romantically inclined poets and composers (not to mention paranoic dictators) have seized on the Valhalla-Valkyrie conceptions and twisted them after their own liking. Gray, Wagner and Hitler have all played some part in misrepresenting both the Old English and Old Norse conception of Woden-Odinn as a god of the dead. We have now to try to estimate how our English forefathers really regarded Woden in this aspect of his godhead. But before doing so it is necessary to disentangle Wodenaz from Tiwaz, for the problem is made the more difficult by Woden's having assumed some of the attributes of the old Sky Father.

At the beginning of the Christian era, just as Christ was locked in a life and death struggle with Mithras, so the North West European Sky Father Tiwaz was fighting with Wodenaz if not to the death, at least for supremacy. As we have seen, Wodenaz won and the Sky Father was pushed very much into the background. The outline of the development appears to have been this: by the first century AD many North West European tribes accepted Tiwaz and Wodenaz as equals. The Roman historian Tacitus links them together in his *Annals* when he says of two North West European peoples:

> that same summer [AD 58] the Hermunduri and Chatti fought a great battle. They both wanted to grab hold of the rich salt-producing river flowing between them. . . . The Chatti were defeated and with catastrophic results. For each side, in the event of victory, had dedicated the other to Tiwaz and Wodenaz [Mars and Mercury]. This vow meant that every man-jack of the beaten side together with their horses and every possession had to be destroyed.

An even earlier example of this custom is mentioned by Orosius who describes the defeat of the Romans Caepio and Mallius by the Cimbri (a tribe from Jutland) in 105 BC. Orosius says that the Cimbri:

> captured both Roman camps and a huge booty. They proceeded to destroy everything they could lay hands on in fulfilment of a novel and unusual vow: all clothing was ripped in pieces and cast away; gold and silver were flung into the river; the war-coats of the men were hacked to bits; the horses' harness destroyed; the horses themselves were drowned under; the men were strung up on trees with nooses round their necks, so that no booty remained for the victor nor was any pity shown to the vanquished.

This particular battle was fought in the Lower Rhône Valley, but the Cimbri had begun their wanderings from Jutland about 113 BC and remnants of the tribe had been left behind in Jutland as we know from an account of an embassy they sent to the Roman emperor Augustus, in AD 5. It was from Cimbraic territory, from central Jutland, that there came in May 1950 a most dramatic reminder of the customs of our pagan forefathers. Workers cutting peat in the Tollund bog uncovered

61   the well-preserved body of a man, middle aged or more; it looked at first as though a murder had recently been committed. Before long, however, it became apparent that this North West European had been held in pickle by the bog, and it was in fact some two thousand years since he had lived and breathed. The appearance and conditions under which the body was found afforded striking parallels to those mentioned of the sacrificed prisoners described by Orosius in the passage quoted above. Tollund Man had been hanged: the rope of two plaited leather thongs was still round his neck. Then, except for a leather cap and a leather belt about his waist, he was stark naked. Many other such bodies have been found in the Tollund bog, many are naked, many have the rope which hanged them round their necks and many are wounded. Professor P. V. Glob of Aarhus University, Denmark, wrote of the discovery that 'the general belief is that such naked hangings were ritual sacrifices in connection with the great spring fertility festival of antiquity'. I contend that in the case of Tollund Man the evidence is conclu-

61 Tollund Man: head of the hanged man taken from Tollund Bog, Denmark.
Found by peat-cutters in May 1950, the corpse was so well preserved that the finders
fetched the police. But Tollund Man had been sacrificed more than a thousand years
before, possibly to the god of war after a battle.

sively in favour of a sacrifice of prisoners after a battle. He was discovered hanged, naked, along with others some of whom were wounded, in central Jutland the home of the Cimbri. Some ten years after the Cimbri left their home we hear of their dedicating prisoners to a ritual destruction by hanging: it is unreasonable to suppose that the Cimbri at home, ten years earlier did not observe such tribal customs. We know from Tacitus that two North West European tribes were well able to vow each other's destruction through sacrifice to Wodenaz and Tiwaz: the enemy did not need to be Roman or some other non-North West European people. We are not told specifically that the Cimbri sacrificed their prisoners and booty to Wodenaz and Tiwaz, but the circumstantial evidence points to their having done so. The traditional mode of sacrifice to Wodenaz was by hanging and the observations of Tacitus and Orosius make it not out of place to believe that the Cimbri intended the total destruction of Caepio's and Mallius' men and booty as an oblation to Wodenaz and Tiwaz. We may conclude, then, that by the first century B C Wodenaz was already challenging Tiwaz for precedence.

There is some slight evidence that the first English invaders of Britain practised this rite of total immolation of an enemy and its *matériel* judging from certain entries in the *Anglo-Saxon Chronicle*, especially that for the year A D 491:

> This year Ælla and Cissa lay siege to Pevensey and slaughtered everybody living there: not one single Briton was allowed to remain alive.

That Wodenaz was gaining ground over Tiwaz by A D 98 has already been suggested and Tacitus' remark put forward as evidence that

> above all gods [the Germani] worship Mercury and count it no sin to win his favour on certain days with human sacrifices.

Gudmund Schütte in *Our Forefathers* has argued that by this time, A D 98, only the western group of the North West European peoples were accepting Wodenaz as chief god, and that the northern boundary of his influence would be roughly the 52nd parallel running from the Rhine mouth to the Middle Elbe.

The cult of Wodenaz spread ever northwards: in Chapter 5 of *Ynglinga saga*, Snorri Sturluson traces the journeying of Odinn north from Saxony to Fyen in Denmark, to Sigtuna on the Uppsala Fiord in Sweden whence the cult travelled west and south-west.

As far as the Northmen are concerned, Wodenaz under his northern name Odinn reached the height of his power in the Migration Age. It is here that we may be sure of the inexorable influence of environment on mythopoeic thought: Odinn developed as he did because of the warlike way of life followed by his adherents the Vikings. The influence of environment on myth is axiomatic. Take as an example, in Henri Frankfort's *Before Philosophy*, the contrast of the early Egyptian and Mesopotamian views of the universe caused on the one hand by the regularity of the beneficent Nile flood and on the other by the irregular destructive flooding of the Tigris and Euphrates:

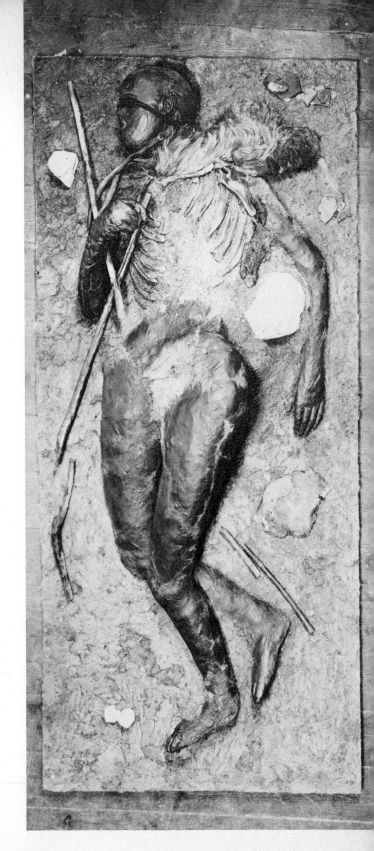

62 Another body from a
Danish bog which supports
the authenticity of Tacitus'
comments on the way of life
and death of our ancestors.
The Windeby girl lay naked,
with her hair shaven,
blindfolded and apparently
drowned by being forced
under water and kept there
under a hurdle and a huge
stone: a punishment, says
Tacitus, reserved for those
taken in adultery.

Throughout Mesopotamian texts we hear overtones of anxiety which seem to express a haunting fear that the unaccountable and turbulent powers may at any time bring disaster to human society. But in Egypt the gods were powerful without being violent. Nature presented itself as an established order in which changes were either superficial and insignificant or an unfolding in time of what had been preordained from the beginning.

Because the Vikings were making their way in life primarily by force of arms, Odinn's warlike aspect is emphasized; but it is an aspect which grew naturally out of his earlier character of god of the dead, for he becomes first and foremost a god of the dead killed in battle. It is his old character of leader of souls with a new twist: the souls he leads are those of warriors for whom he has prepared a special heaven, Valhalla. In fact, Valhalla has become exclusive, for it is necessary to have died a brave death in battle in order to get past Valgrind its entry port.

We have now to try to decide how far (if at all) Anglo-Saxon Woden developed into a lord of Valhalla. The Norse name *Valhöll* would be *Wælheall* in Old English. No record of *Wælheall* has come down to us but that is not conclusive evidence of the term's never having existed in Anglo-Saxon. Indeed, a case for it could be made out on the analogy of an Old English word which *is* recorded and which corresponds to the Old Norse *valkyrja* or Valkyrie. This word occurs in Old English as *wælcyrge* where by the tenth century at least (as one might expect) the *wælcyrge* was linked with witches and other malefactors as an enemy of the Christian God. This tradition was tough enough to be recorded as late as the fourteenth century when the word turns up in the poem called *Cleanness* in the phrase *wychez and walkyries*. It is beyond reasonable doubt that such beings are referred to in the *Charm* 'Against Rheumatism', *With Færstice*:

> Loud were they, lo! loud, when they rode over the
>   gravelow
> fierce were they, when over the land they rode. . . .
> I stood under a light linden shield
> When the mighty women betrayed their power
> and yelling hurled their spears. . . .

These are creatures similar to the witch-wives of Harald Hardradi's saga, they are connected with death and the grave, they ride noisily and fiercely over the land, yelling as they go.

In the eighth and tenth centuries we find Old English manuscripts glossing 'wælcyrge' for 'Erinyes', the ancient Greek Furies. This gloss suggests that the Old English *wælcyrge* was something quite different from the conventional Valkyrie of the Viking Age; and that, even when we make allowances for the bedevilling of the creature by Christian writers, the original *wælcyrge* was a much darker and bloodthirstier being than one of 'Odinn's maids'. For if *wælcyrge* is equivalent to Erinyes, then we must remember that the Erinyes were old, older than the gods who came to power with Zeus; their skins were black, their garments grey; they were three in number but could be invoked together as a single being, an Erinyes; their voice was often like the lowing of cattle, but usually their approach was heralded by a babble of barking for they were bitches; their home was below the earth in the Underworld. Such creatures are much more akin to the 'pitch-black hounds with staring hideous eyes' which belled their way through the darksome woods between Peterborough and Stamford.

What evidence remains points to the Old English *wælcyrge* never having developed into the dignified warrior woman of the Viking Age: so it becomes very doubtful whether the Old English ever entertained the idea of a *wælheall*, a hall of the slain, either. In fact, that familiar spirit of Odinn, the raven, haunter of battlefields, was called *wælceasega* 'chooser of the slain' by the Anglo-Saxon composer of the poem *Exodus*. It is much more likely than otherwise that the Valkyries who were associated with the Wodenaz of the early centuries of our era were made manifest as ravens and wolves: these are the noisy familiars of the primitive god of the dead, the leader of lost souls on dark and windy nights. They may at first have been regarded as the souls themselves, or more likely, if we are to accept the analogy of the Furies, they were the tormentors or spirits of retribution on the souls. And if we are to believe such evidence as we have already found about the Wild Hunt in the *Anglo-Saxon Chronicle*, then the myth never developed much further with our pagan ancestors.

The Woden of the Old English never became the warrior-king in golden helmet, exclusive patron of princes and jarls, such as Snorri depicted in his *Edda*: he was never preoccupied with the problem of organizing his battalions of slain into a doomed army to oppose the Children of Muspell at the Ragnarök. Instead, the Anglo-Saxon Woden stalked the rolling downland, one-eyed and wise beyond all knowing in cloak and hood when the weather was fine, stopping at cross-roads to *58* recognize his own dangling from the gallows; but on black and stormy nights he racketed across the sky at the head of his wild hunt of lost and noisy souls.

63 Jupiter Dolichenus (the Hittite weather god) finds his way to Britain. This altar from Piersbridge, Teeside has an inscription reading IOM (Iovi Optimo Maximo) Dolyche(no) (I)ul(ius) Valentin(us), ord(inatus) Ger(mania) su(periori) ex iussu ipsiu(s) posuit pro se (e)t suis . . . 'Julius Valentinus, centurion, from Upper [Southern] Germany, erected this altar to Jupiter Dolichenus at his own command . . .'. The eagle associated with this god is also seen in Ill. 64.

The memory of the rollicking, irascible strong god Thunor, the divine epitome of all hot-tempered red-haired people, has been effectively erased from written Old English records: but his former importance is attested by his having had the fifth day of the week named after him and by the many place-names compounded with Thunor. He has left more traces on the English countryside occupied by the East, South and West Saxons than any other god.

Thunor means 'thunder'. The god was christened (if the verb is permissible) in the Lower Rhineland although one could not say that he was born there. It was at a time when Saxons and Celts were rubbing shoulders: they traded goods, they traded ideas and they traded gods. The name Thunor I take to come from the second element of Celtic Jupiter *Tanarus*, the 'Thundering Jupiter' and it must have been adopted into a Saxon dialect during the period before the North West European Sound Shift, that is, before A D 1.

In most primitive mythological systems the main features of men's environment appear to be embodied in their gods: nearly all have a sky god, a storm or weather god and an earth god or goddess. Often the characteristics of the one fade into and coalesce with those of another. This is especially easy in the case of the sky and weather gods. The early development of Thunor seems to have been as follows. As a weather god he can trace his lineage back to Indo-European times: apart from all the North West European tribes having a weather god, others of the Indo-European complex such as Hindus and Hittites have weather gods with strikingly similar attributes. For instance, the description and exploits of the Hindu god Indra fit Norse Thor exactly: both have red hair and a red beard; both are great trenchermen and smiters of tremendous blows; both are equipped with thunderbolts; both are serpent-slayers; and both are protectors of mankind against their enemies. These are not all their similarities, but enough to show that the basic North West European and Hindu weather gods derived from the same Indo-European avatar. But in spite of this conclusion there is no common name in Indo-European (such as Djevs) to which Thor or Indra can be traced.

64 Jupiter Dolichenus. Taking his name from Doliché in Asia Minor, this Jupiter, worshipped by Roman soldiers, derived ultimately from the Hittite weather god (*see* Ill. 65).

65 (*right*) Hittite weather god from Zingirli, North Syria, holding in his right hand the hammer and in his left the thunderbolt. The North West European manifestation of the weather god (Thor, Thunor) had the attributes of the Indo-European forerunner of them all, red hair, red beard, thunderbolt hammer, but appears to have taken his name from the Roman form Jupiter Tanarus, Thundering Jupiter (*see* Ill. 75).

     We do not even know the name of the Hittite weather god counterpart of Thunor, Thor and Indra; but we do know that he came to be
64 worshipped by Roman soldiers under the title of Jupiter Dolichenus. This god actually has altars and monuments on English soil as those from
63 Piersbridge, a village on the north bank of the Tees, and from Great Chesters, a fort on Hadrian's Wall. The Piersbridge altar has an inscription which runs

> Julius Valentinus, centurion, from Upper Germany, erected this altar to Jupiter Dolychenus at his own command.

The name Dolichenus derives from Doliché in Asia Minor and indicates a divinity much influenced by the Hittite weather god who in the art of
65 Asia Minor is represented as holding in one hand a double-headed axe or hammer and in the other a symbol of lightning, and as driving through the sky in a chariot drawn by a yoke of bulls.

For that matter, there is evidence for Jupiter Tanarus' having been worshipped in Britain. This is found in an inscription of AD 154 from Chester, namely *Jovi optimo maximo Tanaro*. In fact, it is obvious that in the centuries just before and just after the beginning of the Christian era, the Indo-European weather god was being worshipped under different names by many of the peoples of Europe. It is quite by chance that the name our forefathers knew him by should have derived from Tanarus meaning 'thundering'; and it came about as I have said because they were rubbing shoulders in the Lower Rhineland at the time with Celts who worshipped Jupiter Tanarus. This cognomen developed, of course, into German as Donar, into Norse as Thor and into English as Thunor.

The Old English, while still on the Continent, equated Thunor with the Roman Jupiter or Jove the father of the gods. We can see this identification fossilized in one of the days of the week. When our ancestors accepted the Roman calendar after AD 300 they named the fifth day *Thunres-dæg* (now called Thursday) after the Latin *Jovis dies*, Jove's or Jupiter's day. A tenth-century verse homily printed in Kemble's *Solomon and Saturn* says in so many words that Thor is the same as Jove:

Thes Jovis is awurthost	This Jove is most worshipped
ealra thæra goda	of all the gods,
the tha hæthenan hæfdon	that the heathens had
on heora gedwilde	in their delusion;
and he hatte Thor	his name is Thor
betwux sumum theodum;	among some peoples;
thone tha Deniscan leode	and the Danish nation⁻
lufiath swithost.	love him best of all.

But I have already pointed out that Jupiter really fits into the series Zeus, Dyaus and Tiwaz. Jupiter is first and foremost a sky god, a Sky Father, and not a weather god. Again, as I have suggested, it is not difficult for sky and weather gods to share or exchange attributes. The Saxon neighbours of the Celtic worshippers of Jupiter Tanarus were calling their weather god after the Tanarus part of the name and not after the Jupiter: it was the attribute of being able to thunder that at this point they were personifying. So we can see that while Thunor was 'christened' in the Lower Rhineland he was born centuries before among the Indo-Europeans. As the tribes split apart they carried with them their idea of the weather god, each idea tending to be modified by the environment in which the tribe came to live. And some two thousand years ago some of these modified tribal weather gods began influencing each other and even taking on attributes of the old sky god. In this way did Thunor arise.

Because the Sky Father was a thunderer, too (as we may gather from Greek Zeus, Roman Jupiter and Norse Odinn whose by-name Thund or 'Thunderer' was a legacy from Tiwaz), it is easy for Thunor to be regarded as a chip-off-the-old-block and therefore as a son of the Sky Father. This is what we find, disguised a little, in Scandinavian myth when Thor is said to be the eldest son of Odinn. This is, of course, the Odinn developed from Wodenaz who usurped the position of Tiwaz the old North West European Sky Father. This relationship between the gods explains why Thor's mother is said to be Jorth or Earth, for the primeval marriage was between Earth and Sky, and the gods who sprang up later on are invariably fitted into the scheme as their children.

There can be little doubt that the Old English Thunor was regarded as the son of Woden and Earth, driving over the storm-clouds in his chariot drawn by two goats while he flung his thunderbolt from mountain-peak to mountain-peak. Many Old English place-names with Thunor also have as their second element Old English -*leah* meaning 'wood' or 'woodland clearing' and it is certain that the Saxon part at least of our forebears connected the gods with trees and particularly with the oak tree. The 'blasted oak' has become a cliché because of that tree's susceptibility to being struck by lightning. No doubt the ancient Indo-European speakers gazed in awe at the riven forest giant after a storm and thought of the god who wielded the thunderbolt. No missile was ever found after the fire and fury were spent, but the searing damage was plain to view: so must have arisen the report of a terrible hammer or axe which flashed from the god's hand and returned there like a boomerang when its work was done. This weapon was old, older than Thunor. The Indo-European weather god had hurled it. It was found in Crete as the *labrys* or double-axe and it occurred in Asia Minor as an attribute of the Hittite weather god, and in the hand of Jupiter Dolichenus. The sign of the double-axe or hammer, a T-shaped mark, has indeed been discovered on many female skulls of the New Stone Age in the French department of Seine-et-Oise. These marks had been branded so deeply that the skulls still show the scars: and who is to unfold their meaning? It seems that the axe, the primeval tool of prehistoric man was considered to have an inherent mysterious power or 'mana', and as such it was regarded as a higher being and worshipped. It is true that the Northmen who worshipped Thor looked upon his hammer, which they called Miollnir, the Crusher, as the one effective agent capable of protecting both gods and men from the giants and all other powers of evil.

As I have said, the cult of the weather god under the name of Thunor began in the Saxon lands of the Lower Rhine coterminous with the country of the Celts. From small beginnings perhaps, it spread among most of the North West European tribes. Of course, there were other manifestations of the Indo-European weather god still existing alongside Thunor in Europe. The eastern branch of the North West Europeans had such a god called Fiörgynn whose name suggests that he was kith and kin to the Lithuanian Perkunas and ultimately to the Hindu Parjanya. Fiörgynn, like many other similar local deities, must have been ousted by Thunor. A god dispossessed by another in the old religion is rarely effaced: instead, he is invited to step a little more or less into the background where he becomes a father, son or stepson of the divinity who has taken his place. For example, there is an old god faintly remembered by the Icelanders before and after the year 1000 as Ullr. His name

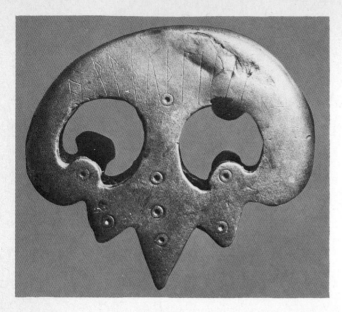

66 Chape of a sword-sheath from Thorsbjærg, Denmark with the god Ullr's name scratched in runes in its early form of Owlþuþliwaz, in Anglo-Saxon 'Wuldor'.

66 is found in an early form on the chape of a sword-sheath dug up from a Danish bog at Thorsbjærg. The form of Ullr's name on the chape is Owlþuþliwaz, that is Wolthuthliwaz, a form which must have been in use round about A D 300. It means 'splendour'; in fact, its meaning is the same as Tiwaz, and this coupled with Old English memory of him contained in 'Wuldorfæder' and the Icelanders' recollection of him as a marksman with bow and arrow suggests that he had affinities with the sky. Ullr appears to have held sway at Uppsala in Sweden before the coming of Thunor under his northern name Thor: names of places near Uppsala such as Ulltuna prove that Ullr's worship was known in the district, while Adam of Bremen writes of a sacred evergreen tree, pro- *67, 107* bably a yew, which stood by the temple of Uppsala, and according to the *Verse Edda*, Ullr's abode was in Yew Dale. Thor drove Ullr away from his fane and the old archer god became in the literature of the north an obscure stepson of Thor.

It is instructive to inquire a little further into Adam of Bremen's description of the great temple at Uppsala. Adam was writing just be- fore A D 1200 and he says:

in this temple, richly ornamented with gold, the people worship the images of three gods. Thor, the mightiest of the three, stands in the centre of the church, with Wodan and Fricco on his right and left. Thor, they say, holds the dominion of the air. He rules over the thunder and lightning, winds and rain, clear weather and fertility. The second deity, Wodan, that is to say 'Rage', wages war and gives man courage to meet his foe. The third is Fricco. He gives to mortals peace and delight, his image having a much ex- *85* aggerated penis. All their gods are provided with priests, who offer the sacrifices of the people. When plague or famine threatens, sacrifice is offered to Thor; when war is imminent, to Wodan; when a wedding is to be celebrated, to Fricco.

67 Thor and Odinn made manifest at Old Uppsala, the site of the great pagan temple? A nineteenth-century painting by C. J. Billmark of the royal gravemounds and medieval church with a thunderstorm raging and a 'wild rider' galloping by.

Uppsala is, of course, in Sweden, and we know that Frey (whom Adam calls Fricco) came to be regarded as chief god by the Swedes. Yet, here in the temple Thor has the position of honour, the centre of the group, an arrangement which points to a time when Thor came first. Just as Thor ousted Ullr, so he in turn was (in Sweden at least) pushed on by Frey.

But in Norway Thor never lost his place as chief god. There are more sites in Norway incorporating Thor's name than that of any other god, just as in Iceland more people were called after Thor, that is to say had names in which 'Thor' formed part. The worship of Thor is even attested on the American continent: according to the saga of Thorfinn Karlsefni an expedition left Greenland just after the year AD 1000 and reaching the coast of North America found itself in difficulties caused by its not having prepared for the severities of what we now call a Canadian winter. Most of the explorers were Christian, but there was at least one pagan among them, an old hunter and crony of Eric the Red. His name was Thorhall, after the god he worshipped. Thorhall decided to appeal to his protector for help against the starvation threatening the party. This is the saga's account of what happened:

> One day Thorhall the hunter disappeared and a search party went to look for him: this state of affairs lasted for three days. On the fourth day Karlsefni and Barni came across Thorhall standing on the peak of a crag. He was gazing up into the sky with staring eyes, gaping mouth and flaring nostrils;

sometimes he clawed at himself and pinched himself, and all the time he was intoning something. They asked him what on earth he was doing there. He told them to mind their own business and not look so shocked; he said he was old enough not to need anyone to mollycoddle him. They ordered him to go back with them and he did so.

A little while afterwards a whale came. The men swarmed down upon it and slaughtered it although nobody knew what kind of whale it was. The cooks boiled the whale for the people to eat and they were all sick after it. Then Thorhall came up and cried, 'Isn't it true that Redbeard Thor has managed to put one over your Christ? Well, isn't it? This is what came of my magic verses on the subject which I chanted as a spell to Thor my patron. Oh no! He has seldom disappointed me!' When the people heard this, not one of them would eat any more but they bundled the remains down the sea-cliffs and put their trust in God's loving-kindness.

We have traced the influence of the weather god north and west from the Rhineland, but while we know the direction in which Thunor's cult spread, the dates by which it reached or established itself in any one spot are difficult to assess. We may take it that the weather god came to be known in the Lower Rhineland as Thunoraz just before the beginning of the Christian era and ended his active career in Norway, Iceland, Greenland and even North America in the middle of the eleventh century. During the thousand years of his existence the hearty, wine-bibbing, red-bearded, hammer-hurling strong god had stalked northwards through Europe, visiting his Saxon adherents in England on the way. In the centuries between his terminal dates his name occasionally crops up: it occurs on the ninth-century *Merseburg Charm* where mention is made of 'Thunaer, Woden and Saxnote'; it is found carved in runes on the seventh-century clasp of Nordendorf near Augsburg, again alongside Woden; and at Geismer in Hesse we hear that Boniface felled with his own hand the Oak of Thor, which like the Oak of Zeus at Dodona was believed to be the abode of the god of storms.

Occasionally, in the north, Thunor managed for a time to scratch an uneasy existence alongside Christ. I have mentioned the examples of King Redwald of East Anglia and Thorhall the Hunter; then there is Helgi the Lean, an early immigrant to Iceland who believed in Jesus and called his estate in Iceland Kristnes or Christ's Headland, its name to this day, but in any tight corner called on the strong weather god, Thor. Yet as Thunor had ousted one god after another in his progress from the Rhine to the St Lawrence, so he himself was finally downed by the 'White Christ'. The saga of Olaf son of Tryggvi tells how Olaf met Thor on the high sea at which the god said, 'The people of this land continued to call on me for help in their time of need until you, king, destroyed all my friends' (for Olaf Tryggvason was a great missionary for Christ, using persuasion or the sword as might be needful). 'Doesn't that call for vengeance?' At which the god looked at the King with a bitter smile and cast himself swift as an arrow into the sea, never to be seen again.

The problem now is to decide a little more exactly what the Old English believed about Thunor, for it is certain that many folk-tales not

68 The weather god fights the serpent. The Hittite weather god, counterpàrt of Old English Thunor, battles with the serpent Illuyankas: a relief from the Lion Gate at Malatya, North Syria.

originally connected with the god were elevated to the status of myth and attached to the name of Thunor or Thor in Scandinavia and Iceland. Since Thunor made his name first among the Saxons and since his earliest attributes are those of a storm or weather god, a strong god and a patron of agriculture, we can be sure that the Saxons of Essex, Sussex and Wessex looked upon him in this light. Thunor's personal appearance was developed very early; there is no mistaking the similarity in complexion, beardedness and build of the Hindu, Hittite and Norse weather gods, and we are therefore right to assume that the Saxons in England thought of him as a red-whiskered giant who carried a hammer capable of dealing with all his and their enemies; and their workaday foes were famine caused through crop failure; cattle-plague; and pestilence. Thunor's connections with farming make for a fertility element in his cult. We can see this plainly in Scandinavia where he is married to the golden-haired goddess Sif, the northern Ceres, another manifestation of Mother Earth. Whether our own ancestors provided the god with a wife and family must remain doubtful: there is no evidence that I can find for it. But in northern Europe he contracted two marriages, first to a giantess Jarnsaxa by whom he had two sons Moody ('Courage') and Magni ('Might'); then to Sif by whom he had a daughter Thrud ('Strength') and who brought him the stepson Ullr already mentioned. The children he got himself are mere personifications of his own traits obviously worked up by northern poets: the Saxons of England probably knew nothing of *them*. Ullr I have suggested to be an old god recognized by the continental Saxons as Wolthuthewaz and dimly remembered as an attribute of the Christian god in England under the title of Wuldorfæder.

The one primitive myth always associated with the Indo-European weather god, either in his Hittite weather god form or as Indra or Thor, is that of his tremendous struggle with a monster (often serpent-like), *68* some power of evil over which he is finally successful. In the Hittite account the monster is Illuyankas, and one of the most important festivals

69 Thunor fighting the
World Serpent: scene
from the upper part of the
Gosforth Cross,
Cumberland, *c.* AD 900,
a virtual duplication of the
Malatya relief, Ill. 68.

70, 71 Carved stone slab from Gosforth Church, Cumberland, showing Thunor fishing for the World Serpent using as bait an ox's head taken from the herd of the giant Hymir (*c.* AD 900). This scene is repeated (*right*) on a memorial stone at Altuna, Sweden (*c.* AD 1000).

of the Hittite calendar involved the recital or acting of the combat between the weather god and Illuyankas. This *purulli*-festival (as it is called) was considered so important that King Mursilis II left a campaign half done in order to return to his capital to celebrate the ritual. The name *purulli* is significant for it means 'of the earth' and serves to emphasize the connection with the mana or power which Thunor himself derives from the earth: in Norse myth this mana is called *jarðarmegin* or 'earth power', while Thor is said to be a son of Earth. The slaying of the Monster is a typical new-year myth of the sort represented not only by the slaying of the World Serpent by Thor but also by our own Mummers' Play. It is essentially a killing of a force of evil by a divine hero in ritual combat, and was at first (when acted or recited) a piece of sympathetic magic designed to bring about the events it was representing, namely to re-invigorate the earth after the stagnation and death of winter.

It is inconceivable that Thunor's fight with a monster should not be current among the Saxons in England. There is no shadow of a doubt that the tale was known in the north of England as late as AD 900, for a carved panel in Gosforth Church, Cumberland, actually depicts a scene from it. The obvious explanation is that this northern version of Thunor's fight with the World Serpent, known to the Northmen as Jormungand or Midgard's Worm, was imported by Vikings, since they had captured York in 867, and though Alfred the Great held them in check, he had at the Treaty of Wedmore to relinquish all the north of England beyond a line from London to Chester. It was during the period of Norse settlement that the Gosforth Cross came to be carved, and though one may argue that the cross itself is a Christian symbol and that Christian scenes are also carved on it indicating a powerful English influence on the invading Vikings, nevertheless the carving of Thunor's fishing for the World Serpent (using an ox's head for bait) has in all probability to be accepted as a reimportation. The most delightful version of Thor's encounter with the World Serpent (which was supposed to lie in the sea encircling the earth with its tail in its mouth), is told by Snorri Sturluson in the *Prose Edda*. The irony, humour and sophistication are all Snorri's, but the bones of the story are ancient:

> Thor left the shores of Midgard disguised as a young blade and on a certain evening arrived at a giant's called Hymir. Thor stayed the night with him as a lodger. At daybreak, Hymir got out of bed, dressed and fettled his row boat to put to sea fishing. Thor too sprang up and quickly got ready, asking Hymir to let him row the boat in the sea with him. Hymir said he couldn't see his being much help, so small and youthful as he was, 'and you'll freeze if I stay as long and as far out as I am in the habit of doing'. Thor replied if that was so Hymir should be sure to row as far as he pleased from the shore for Thor didn't think he would be the first to ask to row back. In fact, Thor was so consumed with rage at the giant that he was ready at any moment to let his hammer crash down on him: but he held himself in since he firmly intended to try his strength in another quarter.
>
> He asked Hymir what to use for bait and Hymir grunted he must see to himself for bait. Thor turned at once to where he saw a herd of oxen belonging to Hymir. He grabbed the biggest ox called Himinhriod Heaven-

72 The World Serpent at the end of Thor's fishing-line, an ox's head for bait.
The Serpent was doomed to lie in the ocean encircling the world till the Ragnarök,
his tail in his jaws. Should the tail ever be pulled out of the jaws, universal calamity
would follow.

springer, cut off its head and went with it to the shore; by which time Hymir
was launching the boat. Thor leapt aboard, made himself comfortable in the
bottom, picked up a pair of oars and started to row. In spite of his efforts at
pulling, they seemed to Hymir to be crawling along. Hymir rowed forrard
in the prow and did his best to speed up the strokes. At last he said they were
come to the fishing banks where he usually angled for flat-fish, but Thor
protested he wanted to row much farther out: so they pulled on smartly for
a bit. Again Hymir spoke: they had come so far out it was dangerous to
hang about there on account of the World Serpent; and again Thor
answered they ought to keep rowing for a spell. He got his way and
Hymir took it good-humouredly. Thor at last dropped his oars and busied
himself with a fishing rod, rather a huge one, nor was the hook either small
or weak. Thor fastened the ox's head on to his hook and cast it over the
side, when the hook sank to the bottom of the sea.

Now I'll let you into a secret: in their previous encounter, the World
Serpent's belly hadn't really fooled Thor when he tried to lift it in the guise
of a cat from the ground. But Loki of Outgard had indeed made him into a
laughing-stock. Well, now it was the turn of the World Serpent to swallow
the bait in the shape of the ox's head; but the fish-hook stuck in his gullet and
when the serpent realized it he threshed about so monstrously that Thor's
wrists were skinned along the gunwale. This made the god fizz with rage
and he called up all his divine power and dug in with his heels, bracing both
feet so hard against the boat bottom that he hauled the serpent up to the
side!

I can tell you this for a fact: nobody ever saw a more blood-freezing
sight than Thor did, as his eyes goggled down at the serpent and the Great
Worm from below glared up and blew a cloud of poison. At that, they
say the giant Hymir blenched, then turned yellow in his terror, what with
the sea swashing into the boat and out of the boat! But Thor grabbed his
hammer and flung it above his head just as Hymir fumbled for the knife he
used for chopping bait and hacked Thor's fishing rod overboard!

The serpent sank down into the depths of the sea.

But Thor cast his hammer after it, and some people think he would have
liked its head and horns. I myself believe it is true to say that the World

Serpent still lives and lies weltering at the bottom of the Ocean. Still, Thor raised his fist in a mad mortification and made a dead set at Hymir so that he up-ended him into the sea and the last Thor saw of him was the soles of his feet. Then Thor waded ashore.

Here is an excellent example of an ancient myth which has been plainly affected in its externals by environment. The writer has turned Thor into a larger edition of a typical Icelandic or Norwegian inshore fisherman and has gone out of his way to add realism by mentioning everyday details about bait-knives and wrists being skinned along the boat's gunwale. The myth has been more seriously affected in that the outcome of the struggle has been left inconclusive. Actually, according to the Norse cycle of myths Thor and the World Serpent do meet again in deadly encounter: but by this time the Viking Age conception of the destruction of everything has been fully developed. Because of this, the Northmen eventually accepted a re-tailoring of the basic story by one or other of their skalds or poets attached to some fatalistic king or jarl: according to the new twist, the demon conquered and the god died. Snorri himself tells at last how the World Serpent and Thor slew each other at the Ragnarök, the Doom of the Divine Powers: but he also retained many of the primitive features of the myth often without knowing he was doing so, as for instance when he reported that the ox which Thor slaughtered was called 'Heavenspringer' a name with obvious sky myth connections. He did the same in another yarn about Thor when he remembered one of the characters was called Mökkurkalfi or 'Cloud Calf' and that (rather surprisingly) he 'wet himself'. But before we deal with that story it ought to be said that circumstantial evidence all goes to indicate that the Old English knew the serpent myth in its ancient form with the god as victor.

A fairly reasonable claim could be made out that an episode from the myth in which Mökkurkalfi figures also appears on three crosses or fragments of crosses now in the Chapter House of Durham Cathedral. At least, that is the interpretation I myself would put on a scene which so far as I know has never been explained. The three cross-heads are all carved from the same quality of stone and, if not modelled by one sculptor, are certainly from the same workshop being done at roughly the same time, that is to say shortly after the year AD 1000. The scene under discussion, which occurs on all three cross-heads, shows three figures within a roundel: the essential feature is that the figure on the right is bending over with its head in the lap of the middle figure. This middle figure has a wand in its raised left hand and is touching the bowed head of the other. The third figure is watching the proceedings.

My contention is that this panel represents the situation after Thor's encounter with the giant Hrungnir, when a chunk of the weapon used by Hrungnir, a whetstone, had embedded itself in Thor's skull. An attempt to charm the rock out of his head was made by a wise-woman, Gróa. The wand or staff was the badge of the seeress or sybil, and this is what appears to be meant by the ring-headed staff in the centre figure's left hand.

73

73 The enigmatic scene in the centre of this cross-head, which may represent the wise-woman charming a piece of whetstone from Thor's skull, is perhaps made the more likely in view of the pagan myth carvings at Gosforth (Ills. 69, 70).

An outline of Snorri's version of the myth is as follows: Odinn was riding his eight-legged horse Sleipnir when the light flashing from his golden helmet caught the eye of the stone-giant Hrungnir. Odinn's mount came under discussion and a race was arranged between Sleipnir and the giant's horse called Goldenmane. Odinn belted away with Hrungnir pounding behind and only managing to keep up by forcing Goldenmane so hard that both horses leapt into heaven over Asgard walls before the giant realized what he was about. Hrungnir was offered hospitality in spite of the deadly enmity between gods and giants. He got drunk and in his cups tipsily swore to kidnap Freya, the darling of the gods, and Thor's wife the golden-haired Sif, too.

As the giant was rapidly getting out of hand Thor was called for, and summing up the situation, prepared to knock Hrungnir on the head with his hammer. The giant claimed Odinn's protection and under cover of it challenged Thor to a duel on the borders of Giantland at Rocktown. Thor

74 Orvandill the Archer, brother of Wayland, known to the Old English as Ægili or Egil, defends his home in this scene carved on the lid of the Franks Casket. The name Ægili is carved in runes above the archer's shoulder.

accepted and when the news got abroad the giants, realizing the seriousness for them of the outcome if they should lose their leader Hrungnir, constructed a clay man to help. They called the clay man Mökkurkalfi or 'Cloud Calf'; he was nine leagues high and three leagues broad under the armpits; they could not find a heart big enough to fit him until they took one out of a mare, and even that missed a beat when Thor came up.

Hrungnir was a stone-giant: his heart and head were stone, his shield was a slab of stone, and his weapon a gigantic hone. Thor went into this combat with his servant Thialfi the Swift who raced ahead to tell Hrungnir that Thor was approaching him under the ground. Hrungnir at once stepped upon his shield and stood there, but they say Mökkurkalfi wet himself he was so terror-stricken. Hrungnir waited with his hone held two-fisted above him. But before he rightly knew what was happening he saw fire and heard great claps of thunder and then was aware of Thor's hammer cometing towards him from afar off. Hrungnir flung his whetstone at the hammer and his aim was good. The two met and the whetstone was shattered to bits, the pieces hailing down like meteorites, and a knob of rock entered Thor's skull and clubbed him to the ground. But the hammer Miollnir continued on its course and pulverized Hrungnir's stone head: the giant plunged forward so that one of his massy legs lay like a fetter-bar over the prostrate Thor's neck. As for Mökkurkalfi, he slithered to the earth in a shapeless heap.

Thor's man tried to liberate his master but the giant's leg was too heavy for him: nor could any of the gods free him; only Thor's own son by the giantess Jarnsaxa, a boy three nights old named Magni, was able to raise the leg and set his father free. Thor rewarded Magni by giving him the giant's horse Goldenmane, much to Odinn's annoyance for he coveted the steed for himself.

Thor returned home to the Paddocks of Power with the piece of whetstone still fixed in his skull. There he was visited by Gróa the wise-woman, wife to Orvandill the Brave: she sang spells over Thor until the whetstone became loose. When Thor felt it move he was so grateful that

49

75 The *labrys*; gold votive double axes from Arkalochori south of Knossos, Crete, distinctive weapon of the Indo-European weather god (*see* Ills. 63, 64, 65).

he wished to repay Gróa at once, and to make her happy he told her that he had recently returned from Giantland carrying in a basket slung over his shoulder none other than her husband Orvandill. As proof of what he was saying, one of Orvandill's toes had stuck through the wickerwork and got frost-bitten, whereupon Thor had broken it off and flung it into the sky to make the star called 'Orvandill's Toe' out of it.

This story made Gróa so excited that for a moment she forgot to chant her spells, with the result that the stone in Thor's head set fast again, nor was it ever removed.

This account as we have it from Snorri is a jumble of ancient myths, and before we bother to disentangle them, we want to be certain that the Anglo-Saxons knew at least some of them. I have already suggested that

73 the removal of the whetstone from Thor's head is depicted on three Northumbrian crosses. If this is true, then the story was evidently a popular one, or why repeat the motif? There is other tangible evidence that the Old English knew the story of Orvandill. This is in the form of a

74 panel on the lid of the Franks Casket. Carved in walrus ivory on the box-top by some Northumbrian craftsman round about AD 700 is a relief of Orvandill the Archer warding off enemies who are attacking his house. Orvandill was also known as Egil, and to make quite certain who the archer is on the Franks Casket, the carver has cut there the name 'Ægili' in runes. Our ancestors also knew Egil under his other name: at least, we are forced to this conclusion when (in the Kentish Epinal Gloss) we meet the Old English form of Orvandill in the name of the morning star, Earendel. So the myth of Orvandill's toe being turned into a star goes back to the common stock before North and West Europeans drifted apart.

To summarize what we know, what we think we know, and what we suspect of Thunor, we may say as follows: Thunor grew into one of the most completely personalized of the North West European gods. He can be traced back to Indo-European times as regards appearance, character and attributes, but his name Thunor was given to him in the Lower Rhineland in the country where Saxons and Celts intermingled round about the Birth of Christ. Nobody could mistake Thunor's red hair and beard and his vast thews. He had power over the weather and particularly over storms. He was regarded as the farmer's friend and in fact as the protector of the world against giants. He fought and (at first) overcame the World Serpent. Thunor's emblem was his hammer, the thunderbolt or lightning flash, and in spite of his stupendous power or mana (said to derive from the Earth his mother) and in spite of his terrible temper, he was always believed to be amicably disposed towards men.

Thunor moved northwards and, when the Saxons left for Britain about 450, westwards. On his way north he met himself coming back, so to speak, for he assimilated to himself (or pushed into the background) other weather gods deriving from the Indo-European prototype. For a time he was all-powerful in Sweden, but had to give way to Frey, whereas in Norway and Iceland he always kept a firm hold on the people. At last he penetrated to Greenland and even to the New World. Although the Icelandic poets said the World Serpent destroyed Thor at the Ragnarök, this was not really so: mythically he originally overcame the monster (and no doubt for the Old English continued to do so), historically he was displaced by the 'White Christ' as we have already seen.

In England (as elsewhere) no doubt many tales gathered round the figure of Thunor, but they have no genuine mythical content. We can be sure, however, that the main myth connected with Thunor's name, his fight with a demon of darkness, was known to the Old English.

Chapter Eight
FRIG

We now come to a subject, the goddess Frig, about whom little information has remained from native English sources. To get any sort of picture we shall have to depend to a large extent on comparison with Old Norse traditions. It is hardly surprising that most records of Frig in English should have disappeared: the Church could brook no rival to its own mother, Mary.

But at least we know that Friday was named after Frig, a fact which suggests two things, first that she was a goddess of importance and second that she was regarded as the equivalent of the Roman Venus, goddess of that branch of human activity which normally results in the procreation of children.

Then we suspect that the Old English had fanes where they worshipped Frig, for it seems probable that she figures in such place-names as Freefolk, Froyle, Frobury and Fryup – names as far apart as Hampshire and Yorkshire.

Now, the name Frig is a nickname: it is ultimately connected with an Indo-European root *Prij*, that is to say 'love', and may be translated 'darling'. Frig is the darling of the chief of the gods according to both Old English and Old Norse sources, being represented as the wife of Woden or Odinn and as the mother of the gods. Old Norse traditions call her Frig Fiörgynn's daughter. This Fiörgynn is not the same personage apparently as the one who under a like name was a doublet of Thunor: Frig's 'Fiörgynn' is parallel to Gothic *fairguni* and Old English *fyrgen*, words which mean 'mountain'. Again, Old Norse sources show *this* Fiörgynn to be the goddess Jorth, that is Earth, under another name. So we arrive at a point where Frig is represented in the latest traditions as wife to the chief god and daughter of Earth. Now Jorth or Earth is said to be Odinn's daughter and *his wife also*. So Frig is really her own daughter, the daughter of Mother Earth, wife to the original Djevs the Sky Father: this is her historical explanation; mythologically Frig and Mother Earth are one and the same.

It may seem strange at first sight that Old English sources remain for the provenance of only two or three goddesses (if that), while the Old Norse sagas and eddas name some dozen or fifteen. We are not certain that we ought to believe Bede when he speaks of the months March and April as being named after goddesses called Hretha and Eostre: but even if these two were deemed to have a separate existence, we may guess by comparison with Old Norse evidence that they were both only aspects of Mother Nature in her young and vernal dress. The Icelandic writer Snorri Sturluson gives a list of goddesses beginning with Frig and including Saga, Eir, Gefjun, Fulla, Freya, Sjöfn, Lofn, Var, Vör, Syn, Snotra, Hlin, Gna and in addition he tells myths in which figure Nanna, Sif and Idunn. Yet on examination it would appear that they are all aspects of Frig or Mother Earth: seven of them are plainly so (Freya, Gefjun, Hlin, Saga, Eir, Sif and Idunn), while Sjöfn, Lofn, Var, Vör, Syn, Snotra, Gna and Fulla are personifications of ideas or attributes from which their names are derived (for example, Sjöfn, O.N. *sjafni* meaning 'love-longing'; Snotra, O.N. *snotr* meaning 'wise, prudent'); and all these attributes may be easily referred to Frig.

In other words, the Old Norse evidence points unequivocally to an ancient goddess who is the earth, whether she be called Jorth, Fiörgynn or Frig, and who is wife to the chief god who in turn is the sky. By analogy we must argue that the Old English Frig is also Mother Earth: for we have written evidence that the Anglo-Saxons did indeed worship Mother Earth in the *Charm* for restoring fertility to the fields:

> Hail to thee, Earth, mother of men!
> Be fruitful in God's embrace,
> Filled with food for the use of men . . .

a hymn which, as we have already said, remembers the original marriage between Sky and Earth, that is between North West European Tiwaz and Earth, Roman Jovis and Juno, Greek Ouranus and Gaia and Hindu Dyaus and Prithvi Matar. The argument is that the ancient Anglo-Saxon *Charm* for restoring fertility (allowed to live on by the Church because it was one of those things better to change than to destroy if the Old English farmers were to be turned to Christianity) remembered clearly the goddess Mother Earth; that Frig also was worshipped by the Old English and is in fact the one other goddess of whom real evidence remains; and that in Scandinavian mythology Frig and Mother Earth are seen to be one and the same: therefore, we are justified in accepting Frig and Mother Earth as one and the same personage among the Anglo-Saxons.

The Earth Mother had been venerated by our ancestors long before they left the Continent. In a famous passage of his *Germania* (Chapter 40), Tacitus describes what he calls the only 'remarkable' thing about a number of tribes living just after the time of Christ in what is today southern Denmark and north Germany. He says:

> After the Langobardi come the Reudigni, Auiones, Angli, Varini, Eudoses, Suarines and Nuithones all well guarded by rivers and forests. There is nothing remarkable about any of these tribes unless it be the common worship of Nerthus, that is Mother Earth. They believe she is interested in

78

76 Cart buried with the Viking Oseberg ship. In such a 'holy wagon' the god Frey and the goddess Freya were pulled by oxen in ritual procession. A thousand years before, the Earth Goddess Nerthus had occupied the wagon as noted by Tacitus in his *Germania*.

men's affairs and drives about among them. On an island in the Ocean sea there is a sacred grove wherein waits a holy wagon covered by a drape. One *76, 77* priest only is allowed to touch it. He can feel the presence of the goddess when she is there in her sanctuary and accompanies her with great reverence as she is pulled along by kine. It is a time of festive holiday-making in whatever place she deigns to honour with her advent and stay. No one goes to war, no one takes up arms, in fact every weapon is put away: only at that time are peace and quiet known and prized until the goddess, having had enough of people's company, is at last restored by the same priest to her temple. After which, the wagon and the drape, and if you like to believe me, the deity herself are bathed in a mysterious pool. The rite is performed by slaves who, as soon as it is done, are drowned in the lake. In this way mystery begets dread and a pious ignorance concerning what that sight may be which only those about to die are allowed to see.

Of the seven tribes said by Tacitus to share the worship of Nerthus, three have never been properly identified and two of the other four do not occur anywhere else: but what is important for us is that of the remaining two, one is the Angli. We thus have trustworthy testimony that at least one of the three tribes which went to the making of the English worshipped Mother Earth round about AD 98.

But the veneration of the Earth Mother is far more ancient than that. In spite of the superiority of the Sky Father among Indo-Europeans, we are forced to believe that they also held the Earth Mother in high regard, for she is represented among the descendent peoples. I have already made my point that the influence of environment upon myth is axiomatic, and where the environment includes a family system having a father as the head then that is the arrangement likely to persist among the gods. That societies in the past have arranged themselves on the principle that woman is the superior sex, we know well: in fact, it seems likely that until men found out their power of fertilization, woman was always regarded as superior. But among the Indo-Europeans a patriarchal social system was transferred from earth to heaven. During historical times, the peoples descended from the Indo-Europeans were influenced by other ideas which, as far as the North West Europeans were concerned, came from the area of the Ægean by way of Greece. These ideas reflected a society which did *not* centre on the father, but on the child-bearing mother. About the eastern shores of the Mediterranean there had lived peoples who from the mists of antiquity were accustomed to look to women for the shaping of their society: here, the social order was based on the principles of the wife's being permitted more than one husband, and succession in authority and property passing from mother to daughter. It is a natural state of affairs arising from a primitive ignorance of the part played in procreation by the fertilizing male. Only women have children: that is obvious.

77 Detail of carved mythological figures from the Oseberg cart, Ill. 76.

78 The Earth Mother, the goddess Nerthus, represented between two of the oxen who pulled her 'holy wagon'. On this section from the bronze cauldron of Rynkeby, Denmark (first century BC), the goddess is wearing her torque or necklace which was to become a famous attribute of Freya called 'Brosingamene' in the Anglo-Saxon epic *Beowulf*.

Two thousand years before Christ, the Great Goddess was venerated under a variety of titles in different places. Just as the Indo-European Sky Father had his wife (somewhat in the background) and family according to the patriarchal pattern of his worshippers, so the Great Goddess had her 'family'. This normally consisted of her young lover or son or even brother (she had no regular husband), who lived blissfully with her for a season at the end of which he died or was killed. His death coincided with autumn and the doleful onset of winter, but when spring came the young lover returned like the sun in vernal glory.

The cult of the Great Goddess was known in Anatolia, Syria, Iran and Babylonia as well as Cyprus and the lands eventually overrun by the Greeks. She was named Ishtar, Ashtoreth and Astarte and her consort 79
was called simply 'Lord', that is Baal or Bel. Sometimes the Great Goddess was addressed as 'Lady', a feminine form of Baal which was Baalath, Bilit or Milit. The last of these forms passed into Greek as Mylitta. It was from Greece that the cult of the Great Goddess Earth Mother passed 80, 81
northwards through Europe.

As far as our own ancestors are concerned, it is a similar case to that of Thunor's, for the Earth Mother meets herself coming back. But there is a difference: the Mediterranean Earth Mother had established herself alone above male supremacy so that when she appears among the descendants of Indo-Europeans in Europe she is confronted not only with a rather pale northern Earth Mother, but also with a powerful Sky Father. The tendency is for the two Earth Mothers to fall together, although to the end of the pagan period they cause confusion by maintaining half-separate existences both among Northmen and Old English as Frig

79 Ishtar, the Great Goddess Earth Mother, carved (about 600 BC) on the end of a limestone sarcophagus from Amanthus, Cyprus. Developing in the Middle East, she later passed through Greece into Europe and reached our northern ancestors under the name of Nerthus (first century AD) and later as Freya, Frigg or simply 'Lady' (*see* Ills. 80, 81).

80, 81 The Temple of Demeter at Eleusis near Athens (*below*), centre of a famous 'mystery' cult. Each year after harvest women walked here in procession to take part in the still unknown rites to honour the Great Goddess Mother Earth. Those women admitted to the sanctuary were compelled to endure one or more initiation ordeals whose form had to be kept secret. Evidence from Babylonian, Greek, Roman and North West European sources may help to suggest the outline of the ceremonial. The novice had to play the part of a young girl on a fearful journey into the Underworld. The descent could have been made to appear real by the traversing of a dark sloping passageway along which, at intervals, the trembling traveller was ritually divested of cap, ear-rings, necklace and so on (as in Ishtar's descent into the Underworld, Ill. 88) until finally, she was stripped naked. If the piercing of Ishtar by a stake is anything to go by, there is perhaps a possibility that the climax of the novice's journey was a ritual deflowering. There appears to have been an Annunciation in the declaration of the birth of a Holy Child. From mainland Greece the mysteries spread to the Greek colonies in the West (Magna Graecia, Southern Italy) as demonstrated in the votive tablet (*above*) of the Great Goddess from Locri (*c.* 470 B C), seen here being offered a cup of wine by Dionysus.

and Freya. But to reconcile the supreme Mediterranean Earth Mother and the supreme northern Sky Father was a more difficult matter, particularly as there was a cuckoo in the nest in the person of the Earth Mother's lover, brother or son. When the divine father and mother came together in the north one might expect the lover, son or brother quietly to disappear leaving little trace. But the lover was too strong and too important to go, and so the mythographers explain the *ménage à trois* in various ways.

Let us first see what trace in the north there remains of the young lover or son so closely associated with the Earth Mother. The story is told in detail by the old Scandinavian poets and historians. According to the *Verse* and *Prose Eddas* the goddess Frig extracted a promise from everything in creation not to harm her son Balder the Beautiful; everything, that is to say, except the mistletoe which seemed to her to be too young to swear oaths. Henceforth, Balder led a charmed life and the gods in sport used to cast all manner of weapons at him without his ever taking any harm. But Loki, the Mischief Maker of the gods discovered Frig's secret and taking a shaft of mistletoe he thrust it into the hands of the blind god Höder who in turn threw it at Balder and brought him to bloody death. Balder went down into the Underworld ruled by the goddess Hel . . . and it is at this point that we may leave the story, for the Northmen proceeded to give it a twist of their own which had nothing to do with the original myth. Later we shall see what happened. The important problem now is whether the Old English knew the story of Balder – and even that must be left unsolved until we have gathered up a number of other threads which will help in the weaving of a satisfactory conclusion. One of these threads concerns the god Frey and his 'sister' Freya.

Chapter Nine

FREY AND FREYA

According to Norse traditions the father of the god Frey and his sister Freya was called Niord. There is never any mention of a mother and this is significant. The three of them formed a family group known as the Vanir: it was openly acknowledged that they were not blood relations of the Old Norse gods who were called Æsir.

Practically all the extant sources on the Vanir are Old Norse and it is therefore desirable to convince the reader that in spite of the scarcity of native English evidence we can be quite sure that the Angles, Saxons and Jutes were familiar with the cult of Niord, Frey and Freya.

The first part of the proof lies in the name Niord (Old Norse *Njörðr*) which is none other than Tacitus' Nerthus or Mother Earth. As I have pointed out, there is the best of evidence that our continental forefathers the Angli worshipped Nerthus, so on the face of it a case can be made out for our ancestors in Anglo-Saxon England having been familiar with a divinity who corresponded to the Scandinavian Niord.

This argument appears to be weakened when we find that Niord is a god (and not a goddess) and that his dominion seems to be over the sea and not the earth. For, a comparatively late source, the *Prose Edda* gives Niord power over wind, waves and deep-sea fishing: if mariners call on him he is so well stocked as to be able to give them land or booty. An old verse is quoted which shows him as pining when he is forced for a time to live among the fells away from the crash of the waves and the screech of the sea-mew. But while Niord is taken to be a sea god it is agreed that a locally more ancient figure, the god Ægir, still lurked among the whales and polyps of the deep. Ægir had been the local Neptune before Niord came north. *Ynglinga saga* says that when Odinn died he was succeeded by Niord whose reign was signalized by such peace and plenty that the Swedes believed he controlled these blessings.

In spite of the fact, then, that *Njörðr* is a true etymological development of *Nerthus* there are two stumbling-blocks to the satisfactory identification of Nerthus with Niord, namely the difference in sex and the difference in those things over which each has dominion. There is, however, a simple and reasonable explanation which I would put forward to resolve these difficulties. Nerthus, Mother Earth, came from a society which revolved round women; Niord was introduced into a society ruled by men. It is reasonable to suppose that the patriarchal society of the north would not hesitate to change the divinity's sex from female to male: it is another example of environment affecting myth. So much for the change from goddess to god: a change, by the way, which explains what I have already said is significant, namely that northern Frey and Freya have no mother. Really, they were originally one, the child of the virgin mother – Mother Earth – and had no father. When the Northmen changed their mother's sex to male, the offspring were naturally left without the other parent, the missing parent whose sex had to be changed to female.

In those days, the peoples of the Danish and Scandinavian peninsulas lived in intimate contact with the sea, they were fishers and farmers with the emphasis on fishers. Their idea of plenty, of fertility, was not only the fruits of the field but even more a rich harvest of the sea; and so they turned Mother Earth, Nerthus, into a combined Minister of Agriculture and Fisheries, Niord: and because their livelihood tended to become more dependent on the sea, whether for fish or piratical booty, they in turn magnified Niord's seafaring side. And so in the end Niord comes to be regarded more and more as a god of the sea, although we are well aware that the ancient northern sea god was really Ægir with a wife called Ran (the very character, incidentally, of Rudyard Kipling's 'old grey widow-maker').

Nevertheless, even among the masculine society of the Northmen the feminine side of the Nerthus cult continually struggled to reassert itself and not without success. First, as Niord changed more and more into a god of the sea, his fertility attributes began to be transferred to a son called Frey. Nor did that satisfy, for Mother Earth regained her ancient position even in a patriarchal society in the person of the goddess Freya, said by rationalizing poets to be the daughter of Niord and sister of Frey. The final development, of course, was for Freya to become identified with Frig so that the Earth Mother is restored to her position of pre-eminence as the wife of the Sky Father.

It is quite clear from what we read in Chapter 173 of the *Saga of Olaf Tryggvason* that the mantle of Nerthus eventually slipped from the shoulders of Niord on to those of Frey. Olaf Tryggvason was a famous Viking who became King of Norway and who trod the soil of England in the last decades of the tenth century. He almost certainly led the raiders who sacked Ipswich and Maldon in 991. Olaf's saga tells of Gunnar Helming, a Norwegian, who having been accused of manslaughter fled to Sweden and took sanctuary at the shrine of the god Frey. This shrine had an idol of Frey possessing the power of speech. It was in the charge of a beautiful young woman who was taken to be the god's wife. Gunnar Helming managed to get into the priestess' good books although the god himself was not happy about it. As winter closed in the god had to set out with his wife on a wagon to ensure that men had fruitful seasons. A host of people tagged along including Gunnar, but as they were traversing a mountain road a severe storm halted the wagon and

82

83

82, 83 The northern Venus: a birchwood representation of the Earth Mother Nerthus-Freya found in a Danish swamp in 1946. It seems likely that such an idol was drawn from place to place in an ornamental cart like this from Dejbjerg, Denmark as mentioned by Tacitus and a thousand years later by the author of the *Saga of Olaf Tryggvason*, in the story of Gunnar Helming (*see* page 136 and Ill. 85).

everyone apart from the priestess and Gunnar deserted. Exhorted by the young woman, Gunnar struggled on for a spell, but becoming exhausted, he clambered into the wain. The priestess said Frey was now angry and that Gunnar should continue to lead the draught animal. He did so, but shortly said he would have to risk Frey's anger, at which the god got down from the cart and the two began to fight. Feeling he was about to be worsted Gunner vowed that should he succeed in overcoming the god he would return to Norway, make his peace with King Olaf and once more accept the Christian faith. After this vow Gunnar was able to fell Frey; the 'evil spirit' flew out of the idol which Gunnar shattered to bits. The young priestess then consented to pass off Gunnar Helming as the god and he dressed himself in Frey's clothes.

The weather improved and the pair climbed into the wagon and drove on to a spot where a feast had been prepared for the god's coming. The people were somewhat astonished at the god's having been able to pass through the storm unaided and took notice that he was now capable of walking about, eating and drinking like men, although he had few words except for his wife. The two spent the winter moving from one feast to another. No sacrifices were allowed but the god consented to accept gold and treasure. Soon people saw that the god's wife was pregnant and they took that to be a good sign. The weather was mild and everything promised a good harvest. In fact, the god's success was gossiped into Norway and the ears of King Olaf Tryggvason. The King suspected that Gunnar Helming was impersonating the god and sent his brother to him with a pardon. On receiving this, Gunnar and the priestess secretly escaped carrying with them back to Norway as much treasure as they could.

In spite of the new twist given to the story, any impartial observer must acknowledge its basic similarity to Tacitus' account of Nerthus; the bones of both are that a divinity of fertility is taken about from place to place among men in a wagon, the object being to ensure good seasons. At each place where the wagon stops there is feasting. After reading this, we are left in no doubt, as I say, that the mantle of Niord, that is Nerthus, has fallen upon Frey.

But apart from a prima facie case for a Nerthus-type divinity having existed among the Angles in England, is there any other suspicion, even, of all this among the English? There is, as it happens, more than suspicion, there is what amounts to proof.

The name Frey means 'Lord' just as Freya means 'Lady', which tells us at once of the link between these two and the 'Lord' cult of the Near East. In Sweden Frey is frequently called Yngvi or Yngvifrey or Ingunarfrey and his descendants Ynglings. The cognomen Ynglings is applied by Scandinavian sources particularly to the Swedish royal family and may be translated 'sons of Yng' or 'descendants of Yng'; but our own *Beowulf* uses the term Ingwine (that is, 'friend of Ing'), when speaking of the Danish kings. The importance of this name Yngvi, Yng, Ingi or Ing for the present discussion is that a significant reference to it is extant in Anglo-Saxon. The Anglo-Saxon *Runic Poem* says, 'Ing was first seen by men among the east Danes: later he left them, going eastwards over the waves; a waggon followed. . . .' In spite of the cryptic quality of this information, it is clear that Frey is being spoken of here under his other name Ing or Ingvi: mention of the wagon and the journey 'over the waves' (to the 'island of the Ocean sea' or the 'mysterious pool' of Tacitus) clinches the matter. Further, Ing's disappearance is an additional reason for identifying him with the 'Lord' and Mother Earth complex, because both are said to leave their lover for a space to be returned in the new year.

Having accepted this much, we may well believe that there is a memory of Frey in the Old English poem the *Dream of the Rood* where 'Lord' has become identified with 'Our Lord' and Frey is used as a title of Christ:

> *geseah ic tha Frean mancynnes . . .*
> I saw there the Frey of mankind;

and again in *Beowulf* where *frea* is used frequently (seventeen times) meaning 'lord'.

The peace associated with Nerthus by Tacitus is also an attribute of Frey in northern traditions. *Ynglinga saga* (Chapter 12) says, 'Frey built a great temple at Uppsala and made it his chief seat . . . then began in his days the Frodi-peace.' Because of this the god is nicknamed Frid-Frodi (peace-Frodi) or Frode Fredegod (peace god) in Zealand. The Frodi-peace is alluded to significantly by Snorri, coupled with the name of Christ, for world peace associated with the birth of the Messiah is a Christian belief too:

> Cæsar Augustus imposed peace on all the world. At that time Christ was born. But because Frodi was mightiest of all the kings in the Northern lands, the peace was called after him wherever the Danish tongue is spoken, and men call it the Frodi-peace.

In Uppsala, says Adam of Bremen, there is an idol of Frey with an exaggerated standing penis; he is called there Fricco or 'Lover', a name which appears to derive from an Indo-European root *prij*, 'love', the same to which Frig and the Roman Priapus are related. Frey's love-sickness is the start and finish of the eddaic poem *Skirnismal*, which is one of several northern versions of the tale of the lost lover who represents the spirit of vegetation. Where the original sex of Nerthus has been reversed and turned into male, the sex of the lover has to be reversed too and made female. So in *Skirnismal* we are presented with a god, Frey, mourning for his lost love, Gerda, now supposed to be immured in Giantland. This story is worth the retelling for comparison with its originals, that is to say the myths of Attis, Adonis and Tammuz as well as its other northern parallel, the myth of Balder. Unfortunately, the account of how the beautiful youth Tammuz met his death and went down into the Underworld has not been preserved; or perhaps it would be truer to say has not yet been found. Accounts have persisted of how the goddess Ishtar descended into the Underworld but there is a cleavage of opinion as to whether she went to seek Tammuz or not. I prefer to believe that she did (see p. 147). Here is the tale in the words of Snorri Sturluson:

85

One day the god Frey had sneaked up to [Odinn's seat in heaven called] Hlidskialf and looked out over the world; glancing across the vistas of the north, his eye caught sight of a town, where stood a magnificent dwelling-place and a maiden walking towards it. As she raised her hands to unlatch the door in front of her, a beautiful light shone from them both so that earth and sky and sea were the brighter for it. But Frey was so paid out for his pride in sitting in that Holy seat that he staggered away sick at heart, and arriving home he would not speak. He would not sleep, he would not drink, and nobody dared offer a word to him.

At last, Frey's father Niord had Frey's servant Skirnir called to him and ordered him to go to Frey and speak to him and ask him why he was so put out that he hadn't a word to throw at a dog. Skirnir said he'd go if he must, but he wasn't eager; what's more, he knew (he said) that he'd get plenty of kicks and few ha'pence in return. When he did stand before Frey he enquired what could have made the god so put out as not to speak to anybody. Frey answered and said that he had cast eyes on a beautiful woman and for her sake his heart was heavy with lovelonging; he wouldn't be able to continue living if he didn't win her, 'and now – you are just the man to go and ask her hand in marriage for me. Bring her back here whether her father will or no. I'll reward you well.'

Skirnir said he would run that errand when Frey gave him his sword (this was so good it fought of its own accord); Frey wouldn't even let him go short of that, but gave him the sword.

Skirnir went off and asked for the maiden's hand for him.

She pledged herself to come a week later to the spot called Barrey, thence to proceed to her nuptials with Frey. When Skirnir told Frey the results of his mission the god cried out

> One night is long!
> Another is worse!
>   How can I thole for three?
> Often a month seemed
> Shorter to me
>   than half this night to my nuptials.

This is the reason why Frey was caught without a normal weapon when he did battle with Beli and struck him down with a hart's horn.

Apart from this story's having been turned inside out and given a looking-glass quality, and apart from its having been remodelled to fit in with the northern conception of the Doom of the Gods, the plot is basically that of the Earth Mother and her lost lover. Even as late as this, Snorri (who died in 1241) unwittingly included memories of the myth's original fertility associations when he named the marriage rendezvous of the two lovers as Barrey (or Barri) which means 'among the corn'. In fact, a number of sheet-gold plaques found in the Norwegian county of Jäderen depict the meeting of Frey and Gerda: they show a man and a woman who is holding out to him a stalk on which is a leaf or blossom.

We can see too, from Snorri's account, how the lover has been accommodated to fit into the Indo-European patriarchal society, for Frey is to some extent being identified with the old Sky Father in that he is made to sit in Odinn's, i.e. the Sky Father's, seat high above the world in

86

84 Helmet from grave I at Vendel, Uppland, Sweden. This 'head-protector' as *Beowulf* calls it, is so closely akin in style to those described in the poem and to that found at Sutton Hoo (Ill. 51) as to indicate a common origin in Sweden.

85 (*left*) The 'Lord', the companion of the Lady Goddess Earth Mother, taken in 1880 from a bog in North Jutland. Obviously only slight modifications were required to bring the original oak into line with the figure of Frey at Uppsala mentioned by Adam of Bremen as having 'an exaggerated standing penis'.

86 (*above*) Plaques of gold from Jäderen, Norway, depicting the meeting of the god Frey and Gerda. The stalk with a leaf or fruit recalls the display of sacred objects (one was an ear of corn) in the rites of Demeter, the Earth Mother at Eleusis near Athens (*see* Ills. 80, 81).

order to set in train the events which do double duty by representing the Sky Father's marriage to the Earth Mother as well as Mother Earth's separation from, and restoration to her lover.

The Old English must have known myths similar to the one recounted of Frey and Gerda: all the ingredients are there if we link together Ing's disappearance (the *Runic Poem*), the marriage of Earth and Sky (*Charms*) and the name Frea applied (in the *Dream of the Rood*) to the god who assimilated and displaced Frey and all the others, namely, Christ. They must have known, too, of Frey's sister Freya although her name is missing from extant remains. We can be sure of their knowledge of Freya from a reference in *Beowulf* to one of her famous possessions, her necklace or torque called Brisingamen after the Brisings, the dwarfs who made it. At least, that is its name in the *Eddas*; in *Beowulf* it is 'Brosingamen'. *Beowulf* (lines 1197–1200) runs:

87 The god Hermod rides down to Hel to ask for the release of the Bleeding God
Balder. In this eighteenth-century manuscript from the Royal Library, Copenhagen,
Hermod is seen astride Odinn's eight-legged stallion Sleipnir with Balder sitting
above Hel, Queen of the Underworld, recognizable by her 'livid-blue' complexion.
Hel said Balder would be allowed back to heaven provided every creature in the
Universe was willing to weep for his death.

Nænigne ic under swegle	I have heard tell of
selran hyrde	no better treasure fit
hordmathm hæletha	for princes
sithan Hama ætwæg	since Hama carried back
to thære byrhtan byrig	to the Shining Citadel
Brosingamene,	Brisingamen
sigle and sincfæt . . .	(that ornament and gem) . . .

Here, in what is after all merely an offhand reference, the poet has indicated the sparkling vistas of a whole mythological landscape now shrouded in the mists of time and religious prejudice yet through which the golden towers and roofs of pagan Asgard peep. For mention of Brisingamen presupposes its wearer in the background, Freya, 'most lovely of the goddesses', while Hama is none other than the Norse Heimdall 'whitest of the gods' who 'lives at Heaven's Edge close by Bifröst Bridge where he stands sentinel at the end of heaven watching out for the assault of the Hill Giants on the bridge. . . . He has a bugle called Giallarhorn or Clangorous Horn whose blasts can reach every nook and cranny of all the worlds.' And the 'Shining Citadel' of the *Beowulf* poet is, of course, the home of the Æsir, Asgard. The story of Hama's restoration of Brisingamen to Asgard has been almost forgotten even in the Norse sources, though it is limned in a poem called *Husdrapa*. If we piece the allusions there together, some such tale as the following appears: the Mischief Maker of the gods, Loki, stole Brisingamen from Freya, a loss which is mythically equivalent to the death of her lover. The necklace was left on a skerry or rock in the sea where it was discovered by the god Heimdall who swam out to it in the form of a seal, retrieved the necklace after a fight with Loki and carried it back to Asgard to restore to its owner Freya. In this story, the necklace, like the lover, originally represented the spirit of vegetation. It is a theme repeated with other variations in Norse (and no doubt Anglo-Saxon) myth, as for example, when Idunn lost her golden apples and Sif lost her golden tresses. In each case the goddess is the Earth Mother under another name and the apples and hair are emblems of fertility or vegetation.

In actual fact, there have long been two main ways of representing mythically the death of the year: one where the vegetation spirit is a lover (or possession) of the fertility goddess, who dies or gets lost; the other where the goddess herself is imprisoned, usually in the Underworld. Both versions persist among the North West Europeans and often coalesce and confuse each other. It is helpful to consider the disappearance of the goddess in its earliest extant form which has been found in Mesopotamia.

According to a baked clay tablet numbered K162, which can be seen in the British Museum Room of Writing and which was formerly (some 2,700 years ago) in the library of King Ashurbanipal at Nineveh, the goddess Ishtar went of her own free will down into the Underworld. Although it is not expressly stated in the cuneiform characters which, like birds' feet-marks, march across tablet K162, that the beautiful young Ishtar was mourning for her lover Tammuz and determined to

88

88, 89 Clay tablet from the library of King Ashurbanipal at Nineveh and now in the British Museum. The story in cuneiform characters tells how the goddess Ishtar went down into the Underworld, a story which may well have formed the basis of such initiation ceremonies as those of the Great Mother at Eleusis (Ill. 81). Ishtar (*below*) is depicted in this impression from an Akkadian cylinder-seal (*c.* 2000 BC). Some of her attributes such as her 'great crown' and her necklace can be clearly seen, and her association with animals, in this case a lion, is obvious.

seek him even in the darkness of the Underworld; nevertheless, the rather cryptic end of the account and references such as Ezekiel 8:14, 'Then he brought me to the door of the gate of the Lord's house which was toward the north; and behold, there sat women weeping for Tammuz', make it plausible that the goddess was indeed searching after her lover. At any rate, when Ishtar came to the gate of the Land of No Return, the realm of Queen Erishkigal, she found it shut against her and threatened to break it down and set free the dead to devour the living:

> I will smash the door, I will shatter the bolt,
> I will smash the doorpost, I will move the doors,
> I will raise up the dead to devour the living . . .

The porter hastened to announce Ishtar's intentions to her sister Queen Erishkigal who gave him orders to admit her after she had performed the customary ceremonies. Lovely Ishtar then entered the dark, doleful regions of those 'whose bread is dust, whose meat is mud, who see no light, who sit in darkness, and who are clothed like birds in apparel of feathers' – in other words, the dead. The porter led her through the seven gates of the Underworld at each end of which some ornament or garment was stripped from her. In this way she lost her great crown, her ear-rings, her necklace, her brooches, her girdle of birth-stones, the clasps about her wrists and ankles and finally the cloth which covered her femininity. Then, naked she entered into the presence of Erishkigal who mocked her and ordered the plague demon Namtar to fasten her close and to torment her with all the miseries of eyes, heart and head.

Meanwhile, with Ishtar in the Underworld, the course of nature in all living things was changed: the bull did not spring upon the cow, the donkey did not cover the jenny, man would not lie with woman, and vegetation dried up and withered. At this, the great gods intervened and sent their messenger Asushunamir ('His appearance is Brilliant') to the Queen of the Underworld who at his instance reluctantly ordered Ishtar's release from the power of the plague demon. Namtar then sprinkled Ishtar with the water of life and led her back to earth through the seven gates where in turn her vestments and jewels were restored to her.

The account ends with a reference to Tammuz which I interpret as corroboration of the view which accepts Ishtar's descent into the Under-world as a search for her lost lover: 'As for Tammuz, the lover of her youth, wash him with pure water, anoint him with sweet oil, clothe him with a red garment and let him play on a flute of lapis-lazuli. . . . [Ishtar speaks] "On the day when Tammuz comes up to me, when the lapis-lazuli flute and the carnelian ring come up to me, when the wailing men and the wailing women come with him up to me, may the dead rise and smell the incense."'

So much for the Akkadian and Sumerian myth of the fertility god-dess's descent into the Underworld. We may return to the north and to Freya. Snorri says of her:

90, 91 The Cretan Goddess of Animals from a cylindrical gem-stone. She stands between two lions which associate her with Cybele and, in the north, with Freya and her cats; the posture of the three figures is similar to that of the 'Master of Animals' (*below*) except that the lions are now rampant and mirror the position of the wolves and bears seen in North West European representations of a similar kind (*see* Ill. 56).

92 Roman silver plate (fourth century A D) showing the Earth Mother Cybele drawn
in her chariot by four lions. Seated with her is the 'Lord' Attis and over their heads
race the sun and moon in their own chariots as represented also in North West
European mythology. This dish is something of a blunderbuss in its iconography,
including elements from the Mithraic religion (the egg and the snake), echoes of
Egyptian beliefs (River Nile and Isis) and general late Roman allusions including the
cornucopia and what appears to be the four seasons personified.

> Freya is exalted with Frig; she is married to the one called Oder and their
> daughter is Jewel. Oder used to go away on long journeys and Freya wept
> after him and her tears were all red-gold. Freya has many names, the reason
> for this being that she called herself now this, now that, when she travelled
> among strange races looking for Oder: she's called Mardöll, Hörn, Gefn
> and Syr. Freya owns Brisingamen the Necklace of the Brisings. . . . On her
> journeys she sits in a float driving a pair of cats. She is by far the most
> favourable for men to call on, and from her name comes that title of high
> rank given to notable women, namely *Frau* or Lady.

Here we have all the elements of the cult of Mother Earth once more:
Freya's weeping and searching for Oder is undoubtedly the mourning
and searching for the lost Lord, the bleeding god, as her title 'Lady'
confirms; the travelling about in a float drawn by cats is similar to what
Tacitus noted of Nerthus as well (for instance) as of the Phrygian Matar   *78*
Kubile, in Greek Kybele, the Mother of the Gods who plays with a lion   *92*
or drives a chariot pulled by lions. This manifestation of the Earth
Goddess appears to derive from the 'Goddess of Animals' of the Minoan   *90, 91*
civilization of Crete (2500–1100 B C). The Minoans were a non–Indo–
European people who lived in the islands of the Ægean Sea as well as the

93, 94 The only surviving example of an Anglo-Saxon helmet with a boar crest: this comes from the burial mound at Benty Grange farm in Derbyshire where it was discovered in 1848. *Below*, the boar crest, a bronze figure originally decorated with plates of gilded silver and tiny silver studs. Tacitus first drew attention to the association between boars and the cult of the Earth Goddess (*Germania* 45); this association continued with her northern descendants, Frey and Freya. Presumably the warrior with a boar on his helmet felt himself directly under the protection of Frey and *Beowulf* mentions such helmets at least four times.

95 Interlaced boars decorating one of the Sutton Hoo clasps (Ill. 43). Boars were sacred to the god Frey and had originally been associated with the worship of the Great Goddess Earth Mother. A warrior who wore these clasps must have felt himself to be under the protection of Frey and Freya.

Balkan Peninsula where they were eventually overrun by the Greek branch of the Indo-European tribes. Seals of the Minoans depict the 'Goddess of Animals' standing on a little hill between two lions or holding animals by the neck or legs. *90*

Other animals associated with Frey and Freya in the north are swine, in fact Freya's nickname Syr means 'sow'. Both Frey and Freya are said to own boars called Gullinbursti (Goldenbristles) and Hildisvin (Battle Pig). Tacitus again found the cult of Mother Earth among a tribe in the Baltic region. He says in *Germania* 45:

> [The Æstii] worship the Mother of the Gods. They wear, as emblem of this cult, the masks of boars. These act as an armour and defence against all things, making the worshippers of the goddess safe even in the midst of enemies.

This is pertinent to our argument because our own ancestors have left records of their regard for the protection offered by boars not only in material objects like helmets with boar effigies but also in written records. Examples are a helmet with a boar on it found at Benty Grange near Monyash in Derbyshire; while there are several allusions to protective boars on helmets in *Beowulf* (lines 303, 1112 ff., 1287, 1454); and among the gifts which King Hrothgar gave to Beowulf was a standard in the form of a boar's head (*Beowulf* 1022, 2153). From the analogy of the custom of the Æstii we may infer that the boar was a symbol of the deity under whose protection the warrior deemed himself to be, and from the evidence quoted above it can only be logical to believe that the deity was either Frey or Freya. In the saga of King Heidrek the White it is related that a boar was sacrificed to Frey at Yule: the importance attached by our forebears to the pomp and ceremony of bringing in the Boar's Head at Christmas argues it to have been a remnant of some such ancient sacrificial custom. *93, 94* *84, 96* *95*

96 Warriors wearing helmets with boar crests from bronze dies found at Torslunda. The god Frey exercised direct patronage over the wearers; as chief god in Sweden, Frey with his boars affords another link through the Sutton Hoo finds between that country and East Anglia (*see* Ill. 84).

There is one neglected piece of evidence that the Earth Mother-Nerthus-Freya continued to be venerated by our ostensibly Christian Saxon, Norman and medieval ancestors. I refer to certain stone carved figures on medieval churches which have no obvious connection with Christian iconography. These figures are not inconsiderable in size, varying from six inches to two feet in height. They take the form of a woman with a grotesquely enlarged quim usually held open with one or both hands. In one example (the eleventh-century church at Whittlesford, Cambridgeshire) the woman is flanked by a 'supporter' having an animal's head and a naked man's body, the stiff penis and testicles being depicted at the ready. Such overt emphasis on sexuality and fertility was hardly to be borne by an established Christian clergy who, from the time of Christ himself, through St Paul, had played down earthly love, had made a fetish of celibacy in men and virginity in women, and had turned their version of the Earth Mother into the Blessed Virgin Mary

98
97

123, 124

97, 98 The unique sheela-na-gig from the tower of the Norman church at Whittlesford, Cambridgeshire. This sheela, like similar Stone Age figurines associated with the Earth Mother, has an exaggerated sexual organ. It is unique because its sexual and fertile aspects are emphasised by its half-animal, half-man phallic supporter, a throw-back to the Cretan Goddess of Animals. The sheela (*left*) from the twelfth century church at Kilpeck, Herefordshire, forms one of the supports of the corbal table on the outside of the apse.

of the Immaculate Conception. Even after the Reformation, the newly organized Anglican Church and its later Puritan, Wesleyan and other Nonconformist offshoots still set themselves sternly against flesh and the Devil: 'flesh' meaning mainly sexuality whether in or out of wedlock. Of course, the countryfolk, those accustomed as Hamlet called it to 'country matters', would buy little of this self-denial, the permissive society having been an integral part of their daily lives from time out of mind before it was given the polite acceptance of recent years.

As a result of the Christian establishment's prudish revulsion from the medieval stone figures study of them has been sporadic, meagre and the results tend to lurk in the not easily accessible papers of learned societies. The carvings have been given a name which (perhaps in the first place a joke) seems to tie them particularly to Ireland or at least to the Celtic fringe – Irish *sighle-na-gcioch*, Scots Gaelic *sile-na-gcioc* (translated respectively 'Celia of the breasts' and 'Julia of the breasts') usually Anglicized to Sheela-na-gig and accepted by archaeologists as 'sheelas'.

There are at present over seventy known sheelas in Ireland and twenty-three in Great Britain. Of those in Great Britain all but five are in England, and of the eighteen English ones all except that at Royston are in Christian churches. The Irish ones are distributed between churches and castles. The Erse or Gaelic name has, in my opinion, given an unwarranted Celtic slant to the sheelas: the English ones are widespread, from the Isle of Wight to Yorkshire and from East Anglia to the Welsh Border; but there are only three (one doubtful) in Scotland and two in Wales. If of Celtic origin, the sheela could have been expected to be more numerous in Scotland and Wales than in England, while the association with castles as well as churches in Ireland suggests a transportation from England via the Normans. In any case, that the English were so tenacious of the 'idol' with the large quim argues a long acquaintance with and acceptance of the figure. The important points as far as we are concerned in our own underground search for the lost Earth Mother are that there was from the earliest times among English countryfolk a reverence for a female figure with an exaggerated sexual organ, that the figure is pagan but firmly set in the centre of Christian worship, the church, and is therefore numinous or divine. The power exerted by the idea of the sheela is suggested by the two following quotations: 'when the Sheila was removed from the tower of St Michael's Church at Oxford, one of the local newspapers stated (I quote from memory), "All brides were made to look at the figure on their way to church for the wedding"' (M. A. Murray *Journal of the Royal Anthropological Institute*, 64) and J. Albin in *The History of the Isle of Wight* (printed in 1795) describing the sheela at Binstead Parish Church:

> The inhabitants give it the name of idol; but it is more probably one of those uncouth figures which the Saxon and Norman architects were in the habit of placing on keystones and friezes. A report is related, that this figure was removed some years ago, when the church was undergoing repairs; but that it was restored to its ancient situation on its (removal) being productive of displeasure to the inhabitants.

The English never knew the sheela under that name. To them it was the 'idol' or, as much later in present-day Kilpeck, Herefordshire, 'the whore' (a name applied to Freya by some Old Icelandic poets) and parishioners were upset when the 'goddess' was removed from a religious setting: in the case of the sheela of St Michael's, Oxford the figure was not removed from the church but taken down from the tower and placed in the vestry to save her from further weathering.

There can be little doubt that we have in the sheela the actual representation of the Great Goddess Earth Mother on English soil. What may be surprising is that the 'idol' should so clearly retain characteristics which go back to the figurines of the Stone Age and even more surprisingly (in the Whittlesford sheela) association with a zoomorphic supporter suggestive of the Cretan Goddess of Animals. That the cult of the Great Goddess did not end with the Middle Ages but still flourishes today is indicated by the resurgence of 'white' witchcraft, 'wicca', in Great Britain in the last few years. The aim of modern covens appears to be to tap psychic power through the witches' Magic Circle. Once a circle has been cast, the coven 'draws down the moon' said to be the inducing of the 'Goddess' to descend into the body of the High Priestess who personifies the Goddess until the circle is broken. In the old days, the business of the coven was mainly concerned with ensuring fertility in field, farm animals and man. Nowadays, according to a modern witch, with fertility under the control of scientists, chemists and the family planning associations, covens concentrate more and more on healing. Be that as it may, there are certain modern wiccan rites which are traditional with roots going back to the Middle East of at least 2500 years ago: such rites I take to include dancing naked, the fivefold kiss (on the feet, knees, genitals, breasts and mouth) and the Great Rite or ceremonial copulation.

The conclusion I reach, then, is that there is more than enough native evidence remaining for us to agree as a fact that the Old English knew of a cult of Mother Earth together with the god Frey and his sister Freya. The cult made its way from the Near East and the eastern Mediterranean (probably with the Dacians as the intermediate link); the Asiatic origin is proved not only by the basic insistence on the supremacy of the mother, but also by such rites of known Asiatic origin as the weeping for the lost lover and the religious prostitution attached in Sweden to the name of Frey, as well as to the brother and sister marriage of Frey and Freya in the *Prose Edda*; and lastly the very names of the god and goddess meaning Lord and Lady which identify the two with the cults of Adonis, Attis, Baal and Tammuz.

When the cult actually reached our ancestors on the Continent is not known, but the name *Nerthus* must have completed its travels into North West European speech before the Sound Shift, so that we conclude that the North West Europeans knew of the eastern variety of the cult of Mother Earth B C rather than in A D.

But we have not yet done with the dying god.

99, 100 The god Osiris about to be resurrected from the tomb of Tutankhamun. When the 'god' was divested of his grave wrappings (*left*) he was found to have sprouted, his moulded shape having been filled with Nile mud into which seeds had been pressed – a literal representation of the Resurrection. Osiris' festival took place at Abydos in late March or early April, around the time of Christian Easter.

Chapter Ten
THE BLEEDING GOD

The myth of the dying god of vegetation who afterwards returns to his lover, Earth, is told in the north most movingly about Balder. It is the same story as was recounted thousands of years ago of Tammuz under the walls of the Babylonian ziggurats, of Osiris in the shadow of the Egyptian pyramids, of Adonis beneath the cool colonnades of the temples of Greece.

    There would be little point in going into the myth here if I were not certain that our Old English forefathers knew it intimately. Balder's name, like those of Frey and Freya, seems to have gone from the country-side. It may remain in Bolsterstone (a village on the edge of the wilderness of Yorkshire-Derbyshire moors between Sheffield and Manchester sufficiently remote to be left in peace to remember the old gods longer than more frequented spots – as indeed it remembered the dwarfs in near-by Dwarrenden and possibly the abode of Ullr or Wuldor in Ewden). Or again, the Anglo-Saxon place-names *Balderesleg* and *Poles-leah*, apparently referring to the same spot, seem certain to have Balder as their first element if we can trust the *Second Merseburg Charm* where 'Phol' and 'Balder' are one and the same. Be this as it may, I shall try in this chapter to bring evidence of our ancestors' acquaintance with Balder not merely by analogy from Scandinavian remains but from Anglo-Saxon sources; evidence which I trust may convince the reader that our forefathers listened to the story of the dying god in the speckled gloom of their sacred groves under the oak-tree branches with their parasitic mistletoe shining awesomely and ironically above their heads.

The name Balder, like Frey, means 'Lord'. It is the first link between the northern god and his Near Eastern ancestors, for the Syrian Tammuz was called by the Greeks 'Adonis' from a Semitic vocative form of his name, Adoni, 'My Lord'. We have to remember too, in passing, that another god from these same parts, Jesus, is 'Our Lord'. The Old English form of the name Balder occurs in poetry as *bealdor* meaning 'lord': we find it, for example, twice in *Beowulf* though with no indication that the poet wished to recall the myth of the dying god. But at least, Old English poets used the word *bealdor* even as they used *frea* to mean 'lord'.

99, 100

In order to set out the evidence for the Anglo-Saxons' having known the myth of Balder it is necessary to begin with the Eastern version of the story and then to proceed through the Norse exemplar to what we may logically believe was the form current among our ancestors. We may take first the Greek myth of Adonis. As a child, Adonis the son of Myrrha, was surpassingly beautiful and was hidden in a chest by the goddess Aphrodite. She gave the chest to Persephone, Queen of the Underworld for safe-keeping, but the curious goddess opened the box and, seeing how beautiful Adonis was, she did not want to give him back. Zeus was called on to arbitrate between the two goddesses and decided that Adonis should live a third part of the year alone, a third with Persephone and a third with Aphrodite. Every year while on a hunting expedition, Adonis was gashed by the tusks of a wild boar and his life ebbed away with his blood: in this manner he died into the Underworld to Persephone. Where his blood splattered the earth red anemones sprang up and the brook Adonis in Lebanon ran crimson. Aphrodite was compelled to shed bitter tears before ever Adonis came back to her which, after his season down below, he did.

In Greece, women who worshipped Adonis brought little 'gardens' symbolizing their own private parts, their femininity: farther east, at some shrines Adonis' worshippers made a sacrament of the sexual act by giving their bodies in the precincts of the temple to strangers. It is beyond dispute that here we have a fertility cult with Adonis' death and return to life not only mirroring the seasonal death and revival of nature, but when played as a rite accompanied with what we are now pleased to call 'sexual orgies', intended to be a piece of sympathetic magic to ensure the return of a fruitful season.

The essentials of the Adonis myth are as follows: (1) the beautiful young man who is loved by a goddess, (2) his death from a bloody wound, (3) his descent and stay in the Underworld, (4) the mourning and tears at his loss, and (5) his resurrection.

Now we may turn to the northern version of this myth as it is told in the *Prose Edda* shortly after the year AD 1200 by Snorri Sturluson:

> Balder the Good dreamed premonitory dreams touching the safety of his life. When he told the gods his dreams they pooled their suggestions and it was decided to seek protection for Balder from every conceivable kind of hurt; and to this end Frig exacted oaths from fire and water, iron and every sort of metal, stones, earth, trees, diseases, beasts, birds, poisons and serpents that they would never harm Balder. And when all this had been seen to, it became a sport and a pastime at their meetings for him to stand up as an Aunt Sally while all the others either shot at him or cut and thrust or merely threw stones. No matter what they did, he never took the slightest harm. which seemed to everybody the best of good sport.
>
> Loki Laufeyjarson saw all this and liked it the worse when Balder was never injured. Disguised as an old crone, he went to see Frig at Fensalir. Frig asked the old woman if she knew what the gods were doing at their meeting today? She said they were all shooting at Balder without hurting

him a bit. Frig explained, 'Neither weapon nor wand will ever wound Balder, I have their given word – all of them'. The old crone croaked, 'Do you mean to say every single thing has given its oath to protect Balder from harm?' 'As a matter of fact,' Frig said, 'there is one young sprout growing in a wood over to the west of Valhalla (they call it Mistletoe) far too immature for me to ask it to swear oaths.'

The 'old crone' turned on 'her' heels at once, but Loki cut the mistletoe down and took it with him to the meeting. Höder stood away on the edge of the ring of gods because he was blind. Loki whispered to him, 'Why aren't you shooting at Balder?' and he replied, 'Because I can't see where he is; and another thing – I have nothing to throw.' Then said Loki, 'Do as the others are doing and show honour to Balder as they do. I'll guide you to where he is standing: here, pitch this shaft at him.'

Höder took the mistletoe and threw it at Balder just as Loki told him. The shaft flew full at him and he fell down dead to the ground – the cruellest tragedy that ever happened to gods and men.

As soon as Balder dropped, the gods were dumb-struck and their limbs *101* went weak as water and they looked the one at the other with but a single thought in their heads, 'Who did this shameful thing?' which no one could ever avenge. They thought they had taken every precaution. And when at last the gods did find their voices the first sounds they made were wails of affliction, nor could one address the other for the distress within his throat. Even so, Odinn had the bitterest grief to bear since his knowledge was the keener of how portentous to the gods was the slaying and loss of Balder.

When the gods had composed themselves a little, Frig spoke up, 'Who is there,' she asked, 'on our side who will earn the love and dying gratitude of all the gods by riding down the road to Hel and trying to find the ghost of Balder, who will ask the ransom Hel desires – provided she is willing to allow Balder to come back home to Asgard?'

He who is called Hermod, the Swift, a son of Odinn, said he was ready to go.

Then Odinn's horse Sleipnir was led from the stables; Hermod strode into the saddle and galloped away.

102 An eleventh-century wood-carving from a farm in Skagafjördur, Iceland.
While the inspiration for the carving of a monster swallowing a figure is believed
to come from a Mediterranean manuscript, there is an obvious parallel between
Garm the Hound of Hel or even the Wolf swallowing Odinn, the culminating event
after Balder's death and the Ragnarök.

The gods lifted up Balder's corpse and carried it down to the sea-shore.
Balder's ship was called Hringhorni. This was the greatest of all vessels
which the gods were about to launch, and amidships they built Balder's
funeral-pyre, only to find they were unable to budge the boat. So they sent
into Giantland for a giantess called Hyrrokkin who came astride a wolf with
a viper for a bridle. As she leapt off her steed, Odinn shouted up four ber-
serkers to manage the brute, which they were quite unable to control until
they stunned it. Hyrrokkin stepped up to the ship's prow and heaved it
ahead at the first short, sharp shove, so that sparks feathered up from the
rollers and the ground trembled. Thor was suddenly enraged and flew to his
hammer intending to smash open her skull; but the gods pacified him for
her sake. Then Balder's body was carried out on to the ship, and when his
wife, Nanna the daughter of Nep, saw it she cried out in her grief and an-
guish; she was born in the fire and she perished in the fire. Thor then stepped
in front and blessed the pyre with Mullicrusher, and at the same time a
dwarf named Litr ran in under his feet; Thor lunged at him savagely with
his toe, flinging him into the midst of the blaze and he burned to death.

All manner of people gathered for the burning: first, let me mention
Odinn, and with him Frig and his Valkyries and his ravens; Frey, and draw-

ing his chariot the two boars called Goldenbristles and Tearingtusks; Heimdall riding his horse Goldtopping; Freya with her cats; then thronged a great host of frost giants and hill trolls. Odinn flung into the fire his gold ring called Draupnir the Dropper: it had a supernatural power in that every ninth night there dropped from it eight other such rings of equal weight. Balder's horse in full harness had already been laid on the pyre.

But to speak now of Hermod: he rode nine days and nights down ravines *87* ever darker and deeper, meeting no one, until he came to the banks of the River Giöll which he followed as far as the Giöll Bridge: this bridge is roofed with burning gold. Modgud is the maiden's name who guards the bridge. She asked him his name or lineage, saying only the day before five droves of dead men had passed over the bridge 'but the bridge echoed less under them than thee. Anyway, you haven't the pallor of a dead man: why are you riding down the Hel Way?'

He replied, 'I ride to Hel to seek out Balder. You don't happen to have set eyes on Balder on the road to Hel?'

She said Balder had already ridden over Giöll Bridge 'and the road to Hel lies down still and to the north'.

Hermod galloped on until he came to Hel Gate Bars, where he stepped *102* down from his horse and tightened the girths. He mounted again and plunged his spurs into the animal's flanks. The stallion leapt so high there was plenty of twilight between him and the bars. And Hermod rode on to the hall of Hel where he got down and went in to see his brother Balder sitting on a throne. Hermod stayed with him that night.

Next morning Hermod begged Hel to let Balder ride back home with him and went on to tell how greatly the gods were grieving. Hel said it would soon be put to the test that Balder was so beloved by all 'as they make out: if every single creature up in heaven, dead or alive, really mourns him then he shall be restored to the gods. He stays with Hel if but one alone speaks against him or refuses to mourn.'

Hermod stood up and Balder saw him outside and he pulled off the ring Draupnir and sent it back to Odinn for a memento, while Nanna sent some linen and many other gifts to Frig, and to Fulla a golden ring.

Then rode Hermod back to Asgard and related all his news, everything he had seen and everything he had heard.

At once, the gods sent messengers to every corner of heaven asking all to weep Balder un–dead, and everything did so, both men and beasts, earth, stones, trees, and every metal (you must have noticed how these things weep as soon as they come out of the frost into the heat). When at last the messengers came home, having pursued their errand diligently, they passed a cave where an old witch was crouching. Her name was Thokk and they asked her to mourn for Balder, but she chanted:

> Thokk must drop
> only dry tears
>   for the beautiful Balder's burial:
> living or dead
> I loved not the churl's son;
>   let Hel hold what she has!

Everybody guessed that this must have been Loki Laufeyjarson who had done so much evil among the gods.

If we now separate the essential parts of the Balder myth as told by Snorri we discover (1) a beautiful young man loved by all and especially his goddess mother Frig, (2) his impending death, of which he gets warning by dreams, is somehow connected with the Doom of the Gods, (3) in spite of an appeal to and promises from all Nature, the young man suffers a bloody wound and dies, (4) he goes down into the Underworld and stays in the power of Hel its Queen, and (5) the success of a further appeal to all Nature to weep for his return is thwarted by one evil creature's refusal. There is no resurrection.

The original identity of the Adonis and Balder myths becomes obvious when we compare the outline above with that on page 147. But what is significant is that by AD 1200 the Northmen had given the story a bitter twist in that the beautiful god was forced to remain in the Underworld: he had to stay dead. Here again I repeat that the influence of environment on myth is axiomatic. In this case, environment has broken the original myth to bits and rebuilt it into something completely different as far as its meaning is concerned. The reason for this was that from the eighth century onward for three hundred years the daily life of the Northmen had rapidly changed from its more peaceful farming routine to include a roving piratical side, rootless rather, and without the slow measured change of the seasons to give it stability and form. Violent death daily pulled an oar with them as their longships sought foreign shores. The status of the farmer was debased in relation to the inflated importance of the fighting sea kings and jarls. That is why the essentials of the myth were overshadowed by the inessentials which became blown up, as for instance the funeral of Balder which is the epitome of what the poet thought should be the last rites in a burning ship of the supreme Viking. And because the fatalistic kings and jarls together with the poets of their entourages were taking the cash in hand and waiving the rest, being content to squeeze everything out of this life, so the story of the dying god was tailored to fit in; he could not return: he had to die along with the rest in the glorious holocaust of heaven, earth, men and gods which they called Ragnarök, the Doom of the Divine Powers.

103 The first two lines of this leaf from the unique manuscript of the most famous Anglo-Saxon Christian poem *The Dream of the Rood* recall the pagan myth of Balder the Bleeding God and the sport the other gods had in casting weapons at him. Christ's cross is supposed to speak saying, 'The warriors left me standing drenched with [bloody] sweat; I was wounded to death with missiles.' Such a scene hardly fits the New Testament description of the Crucifixion, but it does fit the pagan myth of the death of Balder. 'Wounded with missiles' is a phrase from the *Dream* which is also quoted in runes on the Anglo-Saxon Ruthwell Cross (*see* Ill. 104). Although the manuscript (now in Vercelli, Italy) was copied about the year 1000, the runes were carved about AD 700, nearly a century before the first recorded Viking attacks on Northumbria. The conclusion must be that our Anglo-Saxon forebears knew the myth of Balder's death uninfluenced by later Viking invaders.

hwapan yrre wolleton me þa hilde pincay standan fcume
be dhyrhme full ic þær mid fepælum foy pundod . alledon hie
dær bim þchigne ge feodon him æt hiy lice hræpdū be heoldon hie
dær heapthiy dhyrhme yhe hine dær hpile peste mede æpteþ
dam miclan gepinne . Ongunnon him þa moldichn pyrcan
boymay onbinan gepyhde cupron hie dær ophyrhtan ftane
gefetton hie dær on sizoþa peald thid ongunnon him þa roph
læd gulan uiyme onþa æfth tide þa hie poldon æft ydian
mede fpam þam mazian þeodne peste he dær mate pyropode
hpædene pedchi peorthide zode hpile . feodon on ftadole pyddan
upze þær hilde pinca . hnah colode fazu fæniz bold þauy
man pyllan ongan . falle to eoydan þæt pæy æzhlic pypd
be dealf uy man ondeopan rauþe hpædre me þah dyhtenly
þegnay fruondan gefuunon gyredon me golde ypolfpe .
Nudu miht ge hypan hæled min pelæopa þæt ic bealupaþu
pape ge bidth hæbbe saypa yoyza iy mi pæl cumth þæt me
poypdiad pide yyrde mennin oþþi moldan ytall þeoy mæpe
ge feaupt . ge biddaþ him tohyyrū bruene onme brapngodth
pyopode hpile yoyþan ic þhyrm pæst nu . hliyige undep
heopthiy . yie hælan mæz . æzhpylene anpa þaypa þe himbid
æzpa tome tu ic pay ge poydth pita hrapdoft . leodum la
fore æþhan ichim lretiy pæp juhtene zhymde pæpid be
pundū hpæt me þagepynidode puldoyt ealdoyi oþthi holm
pudu heopon juely pæpid . fpylce fpuhe hiy modoyi fuc
mapian pylfe ælmihtiz god . foyi falle mthin zefæpidode
oþthi fall piþa cynn . Nu icþe hate hæled . min pelæopa .
þæt du þay ge fyhde pyze mannū onpypoh poydū þæt hit iy
puldoyfh bium pede ælmihtiz god onfhopodfi . foyi man
cynnify manzū yynnū . yadomify ealdze pyyihtū dæid he
þæy byyyzde hpædene æft dhyyhtin ayiyay mid hiy miclan
mihte mannū tohelpe heda on hwpthiay aftaz . Indfi
æft pundaþ onfyyne middangeapd man cynn yfcull on

As I have indicated elsewhere, in my book *The Gods of the North*, the Ragnarök was a comparatively late conception, a peculiarly northern conception. And in fact, the Northmen did not entirely forget the original story of the resurrection of the beautiful god. Artistically Snorri's account of the Ragnarök ought to have closed on the words he quotes from *Völuspá*, namely,

> The sun grows dark,
> earth sinks under sea;
> > from their steadings in heaven
> > the bright stars turn;
> fire and reek burl
> upwards and break
> > with hazy heat
> > against heaven itself!

But Snorri was well aware that the old anonymous verse sources he was using told of the resurrection of Balder. *Völuspá* having spoken of the 'bleeding god' goes on to link his return with magical growth and fertility:

> Unsown fields
> will wax with fruit,
> > all ills grow better,
> > Balder will return,

and so Snorri tags on to the end of *Gylfaginning* a significant question and answer:

> Will there [after the Ragnarök] be any gods alive, or will there be any earth or heaven?
>
> Surely the earth shall rise up green and fair out of the sea and plants shall grow there where none were ever sown. Vidarr and Vali shall live on as though neither sea nor the fires of Surt had impaired them, and they shall settle in Idavale where Asgard formerly was. There too shall come the sons of Thor, Moody and Magni, bringing with them Thor's hammer. After these shall come Balder and Höder from Hel. . . .

The myth of the dying god has been remodelled; here the return of Balder is presented as something of an afterthought – he comes back along with the obscure Vidarr, Vali and the nonentities Moody and Magni. What is important to note is that Balder is the only one of the old gods (Odinn, Thor and the rest) to be resurrected; for the later Norse poets were determined to keep the old gods killed off in the new account of Doom which they had concocted. But the tradition of Balder's return was so strong that they had to bring *him* back – even in this hole and corner way.

So far we have discussed the Greek myth of Adonis and its northern form as told by the Northmen of Balder. Where do we look for it in Anglo-

Saxon sources? The answer may be rather surprising, for it is in the devoutly Christian poem the *Dream of the Rood*.

For many hundreds of years there has been lodged in the Cathedral Library at Vercelli in Italy a manuscript book of Old English poetry and prose. On folios 104b–106a there is written in a clear hand the *Dream of the Rood*. The Vercelli book was inscribed between AD 950 and 1000, and the language is that of the contemporary West Saxon dialect of Old English. No matter what evidence of Balder we might find in such a source, even though written in Anglo-Saxon, it would be bound to be suspect, for the Northmen had by AD 950 succeeded in settling much of England north of a line drawn from the Thames to the Mersey mouth. If the *Dream of the Rood* were known to us only from the Vercelli manuscript we could not use the poem as an argument for the Old English having known Balder because of the suspicion that what it contains might be influenced by Scandinavian poets.

By the greatest of good fortune there are still extant quotations from an early form of the *Dream of the Rood* dating (according to the latest authorities) from about AD 700. Now, the earliest Viking raids on northern England (where the poem was composed) are recorded to have occurred round about AD 793 and the northern raiders made no serious attempt to overwinter or settle in England until 850. So unless the Christian author of the quotations from the *Dream* had lived (which is extremely unlikely, to say the least) among Norse or Icelandic Vikings, and had thought fit consciously to introduce heathen elements into what is intended to be a passionately Christian poem, then we must admit that the *Dream of the Rood* is not influenced by pagan Scandinavian sources.

The quotations from the *Dream* that I am speaking of are carved in runes on the Saxon cross now preserved in an apse of Ruthwell Church, Dumfriesshire. This cross is of late seventh- or early eighth-century workmanship and can be conveniently dated to AD 700. Of course, only a small portion of the poem could be carved in the limited space offered by the borders of the east and west faces of the cross-shaft which were chosen for the purpose; but these portions all occur within the first seventy-eight lines of the Vercelli text. This was to be expected for the manuscript poem appears to have had all after line 78 added some time later. We have no real means of dating this addition, and all the passages from which I shall argue are contained in the first seventy-eight lines, that is to say from the older part of the poem which dates to a pre-Viking settlement source.

The substance of the first seventy-eight lines of the *Dream of the Rood* is as follows: while all men lay sleeping the poet dreamed of a wonderful cross, the very cross on which Christ was crucified, now honoured and transfigured with light, set with precious jewels and hung with costly cloths. Yet through the adornment the dreamer could perceive marks of the Crucifixion and stains of blood. Moved to sorrow at the sight, the poet listened in wonder as the cross began to describe its experiences from the time it was cut down in the forest until it was set up on a hill. Christ, 'the young hero', hastened to mount his cross in order to redeem

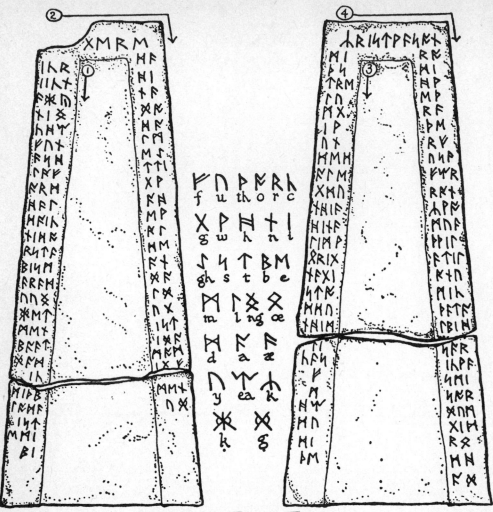

TRANSLITERATION

① IC RIICNÆ KYNINGC HEAFUNÆS HLAFARD HÆLDA IC NI DORSTÆ BISMÆRADU
I mighty king heaven's lord * stoop I not dared * reviled

UNGKET MEN BA ÆTGAD·· IC ··· MITH BLODÆ ·ISTEMI· BI
us men both together * I was with blood bedewed by *

② GEREDÆ HINÆ GOD ALMEGHTTIG THA HE WALDE ON GALGU GISTIGA
divested himself God Almighty when he would on gallows go up

·ODIG   F   MEN   ·UG·

③ MITH STRELUM GIWUNDAD ALEGDUN HIÆ HINÆ LIMWŒRIGNÆ GISTODDUN
with missiles wounded laid they him limb-weary * stood

HIM LICÆG ··F··M   ··HEA·DU· HI· THE·

④ KRIST WÆS ON RODI HWETHRÆ THER FUSÆ FEARRAN KWOMU ÆTHTHILÆ
Christ was on cross yet there eager from afar came men

TIL ANUM IC THÆT AL BIH··· SAR· IC WÆS MI·SORGUM GIDRŒ··D H·AG
alone I that all saw * sadly I was with sorrows troubled * I bowed

104, 105 The Saxon cross at
Ruthwell, Dumfriesshire, on which
are carved in runes verses from the
Christian poem *The Dream of the
Rood*. The runic quotations echo
the pagan story of the Bleeding
God Balder who was immune
from injury except by the
mistletoe. The other gods used to
cast weapons at him in sport, but
Loki the Evil One pressed a spear
of mistletoe wood into the hand
of the blind god Höder and Balder
was wounded to death.

mankind. Many men came from afar and pierced the Lord with shafts until his blood flowed and drenched the cross. The earth grew dark. All creation wept, lamenting Christ's death. A tomb was hewed out of stone and he was buried. The cross was cut down and dumped in a deep pit where it was found by followers of the Lord who raised it up and decked it with gold and silver. . . .

It is no doubt legitimate for a Christian poet to 'use his imagination' (as for example the English Metaphysicals did), when dealing with a Christian subject; but it would hardly be regarded as permissible for a poet to alter the main events and characters of the Christian story. Yet this is what the *Dream of the Rood* poet has done. Where he has 'used his imagination' it has been to draw on what in some cases appear to be heathen sources and in others definitely are.

Examples of the general heathen background may be as follows: references to the cross as a 'marvellous tree' (line 4), a 'tree of glory' (14) taken together with a mention of the four corners of the earth (7, 36) and trembling or shaking (36, 42). It is arguable that here the poet was remembering the World Ash Tree Yggdrasill with its branches spreading over every land and whose trunk began to tremble as a prelude to the destruction of the universe. Twice there is a recollection of the pagan belief in the power of Wyrd over god already discussed in Chapter Four (lines 51, 73).

But there are a number of indisputably definite allusions which are not drawn from any canonical or for that matter apocryphal account of the Crucifixion: they are lifted from the heathen myth of Balder the bleeding god.

If we hark back to Snorri's version we see three aspects of the Adonis myth which have been given a peculiar northern emphasis:

(1) because Balder was magically protected it had become a sport to throw weapons at him;

(2) the bloody wound is remembered: in *Völuspá* Balder is known by the title 'the bleeding god'.

(3) all Creation wept in an attempt to resurrect the god.

In the northern version these three strands have become so important as to impose a new pattern on the weave: for the game of casting weapons at the god is not found in the Eastern myth of the dying god, but is a new development to fit in with the martial background of Asgard-Valhalla and the Ragnarök, just as the Eastern lamentation is now turned into a positive attempt to resurrect the god and is not merely an expression of grief at his death. All three of these pagan strands appear prominently in the *Dream of the Rood*: as I have said, they do not come from Holy Writ, but can in the circumstances emanate from only one source, the myth of Balder. The warrior gods and their sport in throwing spears and darts at Balder are remembered in the following lines from the *Dream*:

> *forleton me tha hilderincas*
> *standan steame bedrifenne; eall ic wæs mid strælum forwundod. . . .*

'the warriors left me standing laced with blood;
I was wounded unto death with darts . . .'

The half-line about the wounding with darts also occurs in runes on the Ruthwell Cross. The assembled band is again referred to as 'warriors' in line 72 of the *Dream*. The impotence of the gods to avenge themselves on the blind Höder (their son and brother) who had thrown the shaft which killed Balder is echoed in lines 46–47, '*My* wounds are still plain to see, gaping malicious gashes: but I dare do no hurt to any of *them*.' The insistence on blood and the bleeding god is marked throughout the poem. It seems as though the poet has brought together all the most evocative verbs and nouns in order to ram home his theme of bloody death: line 19, 'it began bleeding first on the right side'; line 22, 'at times it was bedewed with wet, be-swilled with flowing blood'; line 47, 'I was completely drenched with blood'; line 61, 'the warriors left me standing laced with blood'. Again, this theme is found on the Ruthwell Cross. Finally, the attempt to get all Creation to weep Balder undead is remembered in lines 55–56:

> *weop eal gesceaft*
> *cwithdon cyninges fyll . . .*

> all Creation wept; they bewailed the fall of
> their king . . .

In the face of these parallels between an Anglo-Saxon professedly Christian poem, which can be dated to well before the time of Norse influence, and the eddaic story of Balder it would surely be perverse not to admit to the Old English having known the myth of the bleeding god. In fact, other details of the pagan story were assimilated into and managed to colour English Christian writ well on down the Middle Ages: this is apparent in the disguising of Höder (the blind god who flung the deadly spear at Balder), as the Roman soldier Longeus at the foot of the Cross. According to a fourteenth-century *Charm* quoted by George Stephens:

> Whanne oure Lord was don on the crosse thanne come Longeus thedyr and
> smot hym with a spere in hys syde. Blod and water ther come owte at the
> wounde and he wyppyd hys eyne and anon he sawgh kyth [saw clearly].

It is not the miracle of Longeus' regaining his sight which is noteworthy, but the fact that he is represented as striking Christ with his spear and that he was blind – hardly the sort of private soldier to be serving in a real Roman legion. Longeus is Höder under another name: the corollary is that Balder had melted into Christ.

Arising out of this discussion is a question not easily answered: if the Old English knew the myth of Balder, did they also know it as an integral part of the story of the Doom of the Divine Powers, the Norse Ragnarök? This thought suggests that we are now in a position to try to find out where the Old English and Old Norse mythological systems differed and where they shared views.

106 Page from the Old Icelandic poem *Völuspá* (fol. 2 v.) describing how, at the Ragnarök, the god Heimdall blows the call to arms: the first two lines read 'Heimdall blows loudly, his bugle-horn aloft! Odinn consults with the head of Mimir.'

Chapter Eleven

OLD NORSE AND OLD
ENGLISH MYTH

There are two main sources of Old Norse myth, the poems of the *Verse Edda* dating from fifty to a hundred years before Iceland was converted to Christianity in AD 1000, and the *Prose Edda* written some two hundred years after the conversion.

Occasionally, critics such as Viktor Rydberg have been scornful of the *Prose Edda*, but in actual fact there is a great measure of agreement between the anonymous poems of the *Verse Edda* and the later *Prose Edda* of Snorri Sturluson if only because Snorri based his account on the verses which he quoted freely. He had in addition access to sources not now extant and quotes from seventeen poems similar to those in the eddaic collection of which there remains no other trace apart from what we read in Snorri's work.

What, then, would a heathen Norse minstrel of AD 1000 believe of his mythic material? In spite of what we ourselves know of the disappearance of old gods and the entry of new ones, the modification of old native myths by new tales from other lands or by local environment, we can safely believe that the minstrel would regard his mythology as having a beginning, middle and end. We find such a rounded scheme in the eddaic poems called *Völuspá* and the *Lay of Vafthrudnir* as well as in   *106* the *Prose Edda*: the beginning deals with Creation, the middle tells stories of the gods, and the end recounts the Doom of the Divine Powers. Here is what the minstrel might believe.

The one who was there from the beginning of time was called Allfather. In the beginning, too, there was Ginnungagap, a yawning chasm. Within Ginnungagap, to the north lay a region of freezing and fog called Niflheim, to the south a region of fire and flame named Muspellheim ruled over by a fire giant, Surt, who grasped a flaming sword. Surt is on the scene at the beginning of things; he is also there at the Ragnarök when he flings fire over all.

Boiling and bubbling up from the centre of Niflheim surged the great source of all rivers the Roaring Cauldron Hvergelmir. The north quarter of Niflheim was frozen solid with glaciers and mountains of ice formed from Elivagar or Icy Waves, a river which had welled up from its source from time immemorial. Some evil influence was at work in

Elivagar, for poison drops yeasted to the top and formed a hard scum of ice. Where the hazy heat of Muspellheim met the poisonous frost of Niflheim a thawing occurred and there was formed a giant in the likeness of a man. He was called Ymir or Aurgelmir (Mud Seether). Ymir began to sweat and under his left hand there grew a male and female, while his one foot begot a son upon the other: from these sprang the race of Frost Giants.

Ymir was sustained by the milk from the teats of the primeval cow Audumla (Nourisher), also sprung from the ice. The cow licked the icy rocks which were salty to her taste: by the evening of the first day there appeared from the ice, at the spot where she was licking, the hair of a man; on the second day, a man's head; on the third day, a man complete. This was Buri, beautiful, great and strong. His son was Bor who married Bestla a giantess, daughter of Bölthorn (Evil Thorn). The sons of Bor and Bestla were Odinn, Vili and Vé.

The sons of Bor and the old giant Ymir fell out and the three sons killed the giant. So great a torrent of blood flowed from Ymir's wounds that the rest of the Frost Giants (all except Bergelmir and his wife) were drowned. Odinn, Vili and Vé removed Ymir's corpse to the middle of Ginnungagap and made the earth out of it. Lakes and seas they made from his blood; his flesh formed the very earth, his bones and teeth became rocks and screes and mountain crags.

From the earthy-flesh of Ymir there now came as maggots, but shaped like humans, the dwarfs.

The sons of Bor took Ymir's skull to form the heavens with four of the dwarfs stationed at the corners to support it aloft. Some authorities say that the sons of Bor made the heavenly lights from sparks blown up out of Muspellheim. From this work came the tally of nights and days. The earth was round, and about it in a ring lay the sea; along the outer shores of the sea the sons of Bor gave a grant of land to the giants to live in; but towards the centre of the earth they built a fortress from the brows of Ymir and they called it Midgard. They flung Ymir's brains to the winds and so created the clouds.

The three sons of Bor created men to people the world. They are said to have been walking along the sea-strand when they came across trees or logs of drift-wood which they fashioned into a man, Askr, and a woman, Embla.

Odinn is established in his place as father of gods and men. He sits aloft in his high seat called Gateshelf from which he can overlook all the worlds, keeping in contact with everything that happens through his two ravens Huginn and Muninn. The worlds are supported by the mighty Ash Yggdrasill. One of its roots is in heaven, one runs up to Giantland, and a third goes down to Hel. By the heavenly root is the well of Urdr where dwell the three Norns or Fates. By the root which reaches towards the giants lies Mimir's Well, so called from its guardian Mimir. Odinn is the father of the Æsir, the progenitor of the race of gods by his wife Jorth, or Earth, or Frig: his sons are said to be Thor, Heimdall, Hermod, Höder, Tyr and Vidarr. Certain of the gods and goddesses are acknowledged to be of another race, the Vanir, and their presence in the northern pantheon is explained by the tale of the war in heaven. After the war between Æsir and Vanir, hostages were exchanged and Niord was brought among the Æsir together with his son Frey and daughter Freya.

There is among the Æsir a creature of evil, namely Loki. Loki is no relation to the inhabitants of Asgard except that he is a blood-brother of Odinn. By a witch-like giantess, Angrboda, Loki fathers three monstrous and evil beings, Fenriswulf (who is destined to destroy Odinn), Jormungand the World Serpent (who will kill Thor), and Hel. For the time being the gods stave off disaster by binding Fenriswulf (at the sacrifice of Tyr's hand), by casting the World Serpent into the sea and Hel into Niflheim where she becomes the queen of the dead.

It is evident that the gods are in the hands of fate and steadily moving towards their doom, the Ragnarök. On this day, the forces of evil, Frost Giants, Mountain Giants, Fire Giants, Hel and the Underworld Dead all led by Loki and Surt will march against the gods. It seems that Balder is in some way connected with the Doom; his death will presage the onset of Ragnarök and for this reason the gods deem it meet by extraordinary methods to protect his life. But Balder is slain by the machinations of Loki whom the gods bind in the Underworld.

Odinn, ably assisted by Thor, directs the continual struggle against the forces of evil, the giants, and he plays his part as a leader of souls by becoming the patron of all fighters killed honourably in battle. These are to congregate with him in his hall of the slain, Valhalla, there to await the ominous cock-crow on the morning of Ragnarök. Odinn seeks advice from the talking head of Mimir in a fruitless effort to avert *106* the decrees of fate.

At the Ragnarök the demons destroy the gods and the world; but a new heaven and a new earth arise after the fires of Surt have done their worst. Two human beings, Lif and Lifthrasir hide in Hoddmimir's Holt and survive the cataclysm: they repeople the earth. Balder and other, rather obscure gods, return in peace to heaven.

How tempting it is on the basis of what remains in Old Norse to fill in the picture of what we think Old English mythology must have been. It is as though an archaeologist had cleared away the spoil of centuries from two kindred mosaics: neither is perfect, but while the greater part of the one is picture, the greater part of the other is dust. What is left of the broken Old English mosaic shows it to have great similarities to, as well as differences from, the Old Norse picture. The similarities outnumber the differences and it is therefore tempting to fill in the blanks by using pieces copied from the more complete picture. But we have to remember that many of the Norse mosaic pieces are late, having been fashioned or refashioned long after continental contact between the English part of the North West Europeans and the Northern branch had ceased. If we bear this in mind, then we may with benefit attempt some schematic reconstruction of an Anglo-Saxon mythology.

Early research workers into the subject of the beliefs of the North West Europeans assumed that our continental forefathers subscribed to a homogeneous religion which was reflected in such common North West European words as Wyrd-Wyrt-Urdr, Woden-Wuotan-Wodan-Odinn, Thunor-Thunaer-Thor, Wælcyrge-Valkyrja, Middangeard-Midgard-Mittilagart-Midjungards, and so on. It is obvious that such terms are only dialectal forms in Old English, Old Norse, Gothic or Old High German of what were originally parent words in the Primitive North West European tongue. Nevertheless, we have seen already that the assumption of a shared homogeneous religion is not wholly confirmed: and in making use of Norse sources, we have to admit that the *Eddas* are to be regarded as a special Scandinavian and particularly Norwegian Icelandic expression of myth. Further, we note two points: first, that the records of myths in the two *Eddas* are not always complete but, on the contrary, often fragmentary; and second, there are different myths dealing with the same subject not only in the two *Eddas* but also in one and the same *Edda*. An example of this is Snorri's collection of myths on Night, Day, Sun and Moon.

There do appear to be, however, certain fundamental notions embodied in North West European words which go back to the Indo-European level. This is especially noticeable where the cosmography is concerned. It is natural that there should be a number of shared synonyms for the world: we find the idea 'world' expressed by Old High German *weralt*, Old Frisian *wiarlt*, Old Norse *veröld*, and Old English *weorold*; there is also 'earth', Old Norse *jörth* and Old English *eord* as well as Old Norse *jörmungrund* and Old English *eormengrund*. With such serviceable names available it is clear that the North West Europeans wished to give expression to a definite idea when they also referred to the world as 'the middle enclosure', Old High German *mittilagart*, Gothic *midjungards*, Old Norse *miðgarðr* and Old English *middangeard*. The world was conceived to be in the middle of something – but of what?

Another common notion is that of 'heaven', North West European *himinaz*, O.N. *himinn*, O.E. *heofon*; yet another is 'hell', O.N. *hel*, O.E. *hel*, Gothic *halja* and Old Frisian *helle*. According to common traditions the road to heaven is always up and the road to hell always down, so we may believe with assurance that our North West European ancestors, and hence the Old English, knew of a universe in which the world occupied a middle position with heaven above and hell beneath. The pagan Northmen were known to accept a pretty complicated universe consisting of some 'nine worlds' said to be those of the Æsir, Vanir, light elves, dark elves, men, giants, the dead, Muspell's sons and presumably of the dwarfs (though the ninth world is uncertain). We cannot be sure that the Old English did not have a similar belief; for it may well be that there is evidence of it in the *Nine Herbs Charm* which refers explicitly to the 'seven worlds'. Editors sometimes trace the seven worlds to a Classical source – the seven heavens or spheres associated with the seven planets of ancient Classical cosmology; but there is just as good a case for the pagan derivation as the Classical one. If the Old English did commonly acknowledge a universe consisting of seven worlds then which two of the Northmen's nine did they not know of? My supposition would be that our forefathers did not believe in Vanaheim (the world of the Vanir) and Muspellzheimr (the home of the Destroyers of the World). My reason is that there are Anglo-Saxon words corresponding to Æsir, elves, men, giants, dwarfs and the dead: but no reference has remained in Old English to the Vanir or the sons of Muspell. All other evidence tends to show, too, that the working up of the notions of the Vanir and sons of Muspell was done on Norwegian and Icelandic soil.

I take it, then, that the Old English did believe in the 'seven worlds'. Did they also believe in a world tree (like the Norse Yggdrasill) supposed to be supporting the entire universe? Before attempting to answer that question let us first look at the Old Norse tradition. Snorri Sturluson says:

> That particular Ash is of all trees the hugest and most stately. Its branches overhang all the worlds and strike out above the heavens. The three roots of the tree, spreading far and wide, support it aloft: one root is with the gods, another with the Frost Giants (where formerly there used to be the Yawning Gulf), and the third stands over Niflheim: under that root is the Roaring Cauldron called Hvergelmir with the dragon Nidhogg gnawing the root from below. But under the root which twists towards the Frost Giants there is Mimir's well (for he is called Mimir who is warden of the well). Mimir is full of wisdom since he drinks at the well out of Giallarhorn. . . . The third root of the Ash stands in heaven and beneath it is the spring (exceedingly sacred) named the well of Urdr. That's where the gods have their judgement seat. Every day, over Bifröst the Rainbow Bridge the Powers gallop to it; that's why it is called the Æsir's Bridge. . . . There's an eagle roosting in the boughs of the Ash Tree, wise beyond all knowing, and between his eyes sits the hawk Vedrfolnir. A squirrel, by name Ratatosk, darts up and down about the tree bearing spiteful tales between the eagle and Nidhogg. Four stags browse over the branches of the Ash and nibble at the bark. I'll tell you their names: Dainn, Dvalinn, Duneyrr and Dura-throrr. And there's such a nest of serpents with Nidhogg in Hvergelmir no tongue could possibly tell their tale. . . . It's said too that the Norns, who dwell round the well of Urdr, every day take the water of the well mixed together with the gravel lying about the well and sprinkle it over the Ash to prevent its limbs from withering or rotting. . . . The dew which drips on to the ground beneath the tree is called honeydew by men, and bees are nourished on it. The well of Urdr gives life to two birds named Swans, from whom are descended that kind of bird which is now so called.

We cannot dismiss out of hand the suggestion that the Old English knew of a world tree simply because there appears to be little or no native literary evidence extant for such a tree. There *is* evidence of the worship of an immense wooden column by the Old Saxons on the Continent, and there *are* maypoles to this day in England. The great pillar of wood venerated by the continental Saxons at Eresburg, now Marsberg on the River Diemel was called the Irminsul. The first part of the name seems identical with Old English *eormen* and Old Norse *jörmun* meaning 'vast' or 'monstrous'. The Irminsul was cut down at the instigation of Charle-

magne in AD 772. Three days were needed to complete the job of breaking up the sanctuary and the destroyers carried off much gold and silver. The only ancient source which gives an account of the Irminsul is the *Translatio S. Alexandri* which in Chapter 3 says that the Saxons:

> also worshipped a wooden column of no mean size which was raised aloft in the open. They call it in their own language *Irminsul* which in Latin means 'a universal column, a sort of sustainer of everything'.

This explanation of the name is, of course, repeating what the Northmen believed about Yggdrasill.

The Irminsul stood by a shrine or temple and its situation at Marsberg would identify it with what Tacitus in the *Annals* (i. 51) calls 'the most revered holy place of the Marsi' known as the temple of Tanfana. We know of other North West European examples of trees or poles standing by temples with a well close to. According to Adam of Bremen there was a great tree overhanging the temple at Uppsala. Its roots and branches spread far and wide in all directions. Near by was a well in which living men were sacrificed by drowning. This tree was green all the year round but nobody knew what kind it was.

World pillars and poles figure in the myths of many widely separated and unrelated peoples. The idea is duplicated in Norse myth where in addition to the World Ash Tree Yggdrasill we are told of four dwarfs who stand at the cardinal points supporting the sky. South American Indians speak of a World Tree; while ancient Egyptian stories tell that

107

108

107, 108 The great heathen temple at Uppsala, Sweden which, according to Adam of Bremen was overhung by a great tree close to a well in which living men were drowned as sacrifices to the gods. *Right*, detail from the cauldron found at Gundestrup, Denmark showing a ritual by drowning – *cf*. the drowned Windeby girl (Ill. 62).

the sky was an iron roof held aloft by four pillars at north, south, east, and west, or yet again was the body of the goddess Nut whom her father Shu held apart from her brother and husband Geb, the earth. Eskimos tell of four posts underpinning the firmament and when these posts go rotten they have to be renewed by the angekok or wizards. It is certainly not straining credulity to believe that the Saxon part of our ancestors brought with them to Britain a feeling of veneration for holy trees or poles like the Irminsul. In fact, we are probably right in seeing a memory of this veneration in our forebears' regard for the maypole. The maypoles of early England were not the matchsticks we see sometimes still; they might well have been called 'eormen' or vast. For instance, the Church of St Andrew Undershaft in London is supposed to take its name from a lofty maypole which in the fifteenth century overtopped the church tower; or another, set up in the Strand in 1661, is said to have been 134 feet high.

109, 110

111

If there are correspondences between Old Norse and Old English cosmography, how far is there evidence for Anglo-Saxon pagan creation myths after the Scandinavian pattern? The giant Ymir is the central figure: we saw at the start of this chapter that the earth and sky were formed from his carcass while the sea was his blood which drowned the other giants. As I have already pointed out, *Beowulf* recalls the giants who struggled against God and who were annihilated in a flood. Is there any other evidence which would confirm the two allusions to drowned giants in *Beowulf* as being connected with a creation myth in which the world was made from the carcass of the chief of their kind? I believe that

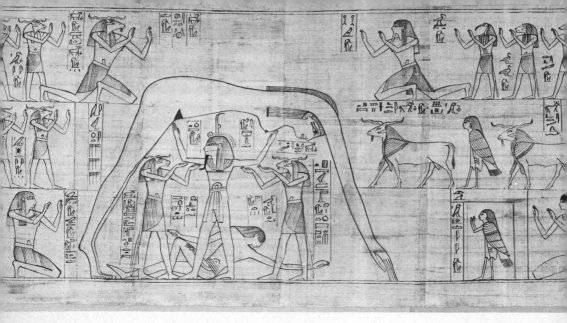

109 The Egyptian sky goddess Nut arched over the earth god Geb and supported by the air god Shu, from the Greenfield Papyrus.

there is. Our ancestors on the Continent *did* know of a creation myth involving a being like Norse Ymir who was 'sprung from the earth'. In *Germania* 2 Tacitus refers to our continental forefathers' ancient ballads, their only form of recorded history, in which they celebrate Tvisto, a god sprung from the earth, and they assign to him a son called Mannus, the founder of their race, and to Mannus three sons, their progenitors, after whom the people nearest Ocean are called Ingævones, those of the centre Herminones, the remainder Istævones. And if we set this account side by side with the various similar tales from both *Eddas* and from Snorri alone, we get three family trees which it is not straining probability to believe came from one single archetype:

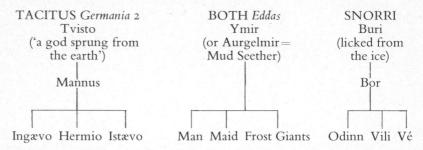

TACITUS *Germania* 2	BOTH *Eddas*	SNORRI
Tvisto	Ymir	Buri
('a god sprung from the earth')	(or Aurgelmir = Mud Seether)	(licked from the ice)
Mannus		Bor
Ingævo Hermio Istævo	Man Maid Frost Giants	Odinn Vili Vé

If our continental ancestors sang of their descent from Tvisto it is at least on the cards that the Angles, Saxons and Jutes brought the story over to Britain with them. That something has gone radically wrong with the Ymir myth in its latest manifestation is clear: for Ymir is made to be the ancestor of humankind at the same time as he is said to be the one who gave birth to evil beings, the Frost Giants. That Ymir (like Tvisto) was

110 Nut, the Egyptian sky goddess, from the inside of a sarcophagus lid. This image perfectly portrays the immanence of the godhead in nature: Nut *is* the sky, and she gives birth to the sun (the disc over her vulva) every morning and swallows the sun each night. Our own ancestors believed that the disappearance of the Sky Father at night was due to his being swallowed by a wolf. There is no difference in kind between these two interpretations of natural phenomena.

originally the progenitor of mankind and not of giants is suggested by his name. 'Ymir' looks as if it might derive from Swedish *ymu-man* 'man from Umeå Lappmark' and be part of the body of evidence to show that the ancient Scandinavians derived their primeval ancestors from the Finns. We shall be fairly safe in assuming that Ymir-Tvisto was regarded in the north as the progenitor of mankind down to as late as the end of the first century AD and that a memory of the myth in its modified form which involved Ymir and the drowning of the giants was known to the Old English.

I would suggest that another pagan account of Creation is concealed in one of our earliest Anglo-Saxon poems which did actually deal with Creation, but as everyone believes, with the Old Testament Creation and with the Christian God as Creator. In fact, editors have called the poem a 'hymn', 'Cædmon's Hymn', after its composer Cædmon, a rustic lay brother in charge of the animals at Whitby Abbey, Yorkshire, and late on in life a monk. Cædmon died before AD 700; his hymn must therefore have been composed in the last decades of the previous century, that is to say, within fifty years of acknowledged heathenism in Northumbria. Cædmon was born into a pagan world and his first learning must have been pagan. There is a curious thing about his hymn: in spite of Cædmon's extreme devoutness as suggested by Bede, it would appear that even as the shadow of the ancient Britons cast itself forward in his name (from British *Catumannos*), so the memory of the heathen English conception of Creation can be traced in the hymn like the foundations of some long-lost buried town seen through the earth's surface in a dry season from an air-photograph. To show what I mean, it will be convenient to give the hymn as Cædmon wrote it with a literal translation alongside:

Nu scylun hergan	Now [we] shall praise
hefaenricaes uard,	the heavenly kingdom's Warden,
metudæs maecti	the Measurer's might
end his modgidanc,	and his understanding,
uerc uuldurfadur	the work of Glory-father
sue he uundrá gihuaes,	even as he, of each wonder,
eci dryctin,	the eternal Lord,
or astelidæ;	the beginning ordained;
he aerist scop	he first shaped
aelda barnum	for the sons of men
heben til hrofe,	heaven as a roof
haleg scepen,	the Holy Shaper,
tha middungeard	then the middle enclosure,
moncynnæs uard;	mankind's Warden;
eci dryctin	the eternal Lord
æfter tiadæ	afterwards created
firum foldu	the world for men—
frea allmectig.	that Frey almighty.

This poem is made up of nine lines divided into eighteen half-lines as set out above. What is most curious is that at least nine of these eighteen

111 The huge maypole set up each year from time out of mind until 1517 in front of the Church of St Andrew Undershaft in Leadenhall Street, London. After a disturbance the maypole was kept for thirty-two years under the eaves of a row of thatched cottages, until the curate of St Catherine Cree, Sir Stephen, preached against it at St Paul's Cross as an idol. The outcome was 'that the parishioners after they had dined, raised the pole off the hooks on which it had rested so many years, and each man sawing off for himself a piece equal to the length of his house it was quickly demolished and burned': a fate which echoes that meted out to the wooden images of the old gods Woden, Thunor and Frey by the converted Anglo-Saxons.

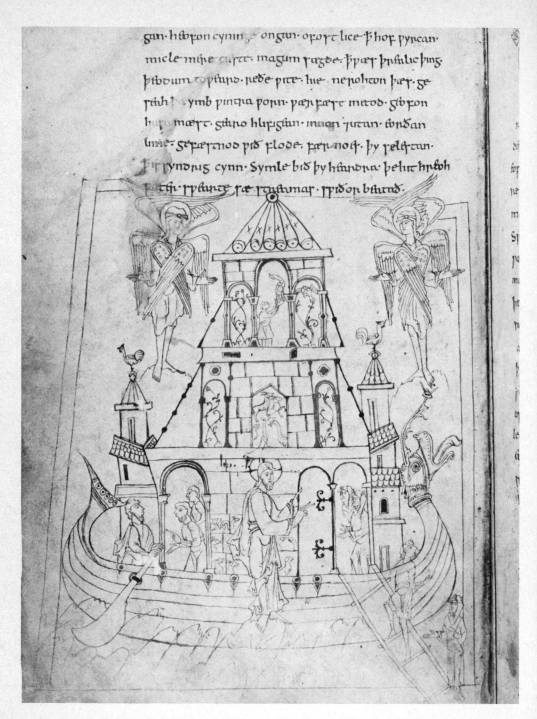

112 Noah's Ark from the manuscript of Caedmon's paraphrase of Genesis. A
three-storeyed ship is as far removed from reality as the hull with its dragon-head
and beautifully shaped steering-oar is close to fact. Was the artist remembering
the old division of the Universe into Asgard, Midgard and the Underworld even as
Caedmon's Hymn recalls the pagan myth of the creation?

half-lines are to be found word for word in other Anglo-Saxon verse. For instance, *eci dryctin* occurring twice in the hymn is found frequently in *Beowulf*; then the second, third, eighth, tenth, eleventh, fourteenth and eighteenth half-lines are repeated in *Genesis*, *Riddles*, *Judith* and other poems. A. H. Smith on page 15 of his *Three Northumbrian Poems* has explained this phenomenon as follows:

> In Cædmon's time when Northumbria had been converted to Christianity for only half a century these phrases belonging to Christian poetry could scarcely have become conventional, as they certainly were in later Old English; on the contrary, the poem represents the beginning of such diction. . . .

The logical conclusion of this argument is that the Anglo-Saxon poetic clichés all stem from 'Cædmon's Hymn' which is extremely unlikely, not to say ridiculous. Rather, these phrases were clichés when Cædmon employed them, but the clichés of a pre-Christian poetic diction, of a heathen tradition. This contention is strongly supported by other phrases and ideas in the hymn. For example, the word *metudæs* in the third half-line is the possessive singular form of a noun later occurring as *Metod* or *Meotod* which is normally translated 'Creator' but which means literally 'Measurer' – it is connected with the modern verb to 'mete' out. Such a title (as I have already said) looks suspiciously like a pagan name for one of the three Fates, the one who measured out the thread of life, later transferred to the Christian God. And even though Metod is usually taken to be a masculine noun this is no real bar to my suggestion. We have seen what happened to Nerthus. Again, the name *uuldurfadur* is a title formed like the Norse *Alföðr*, 'Allfather' or the Greek Zeuspater or Hindu Dyauspitar. But what is more striking, the first element 'uuldur' is the local form of the North West European 'Wolthuthliwaz' and Old Norse 'Ullr', the sky god whose name meant 'splendour' even as Tiw originally meant 'resplendent': in short, I suggest that Uuldurfadur was an ancient name for the Sky Father. I need hardly repeat that the last half-line of the hymn contains a memory of Frey. In addition, the phrase 'hefaenricaes uard', 'the heavenly kingdom's Warden' is strongly reminiscent of the Old Norse god Heimdall, the guardian of heaven; while 'middungeard' is, of course, a word for the earth as the middle enclosure of the old pagan cosmography. 112, 113

I have now said what seems to me can be reasonably reported on the subject of what the Old English knew of the creation stories; I have also dealt in the body of this work with the 'middle' of the mythology, namely, what remains about the gods; it is now left for me to deal with the 'end'.

There are one or two general observations and first, that many mythological systems (if not the majority), besides accepting a Creation, also accept a Day of Doom. This word 'doom' is interesting because it really contains two quite distinct notions: originally it meant 'judgment', but gradually the idea of adverse judgment gained ascendancy until the

113 King Gylfi disguised as a wandering beggarman questioning three gods in Asgard about the pagan myths. In the *Prose Edda* the gods are named High, Even-as-High and The Third and are taken to be Odinn regarded as a Trinity.

ordinary meaning of doom came to be death and destruction. 'Doomsday' was the day of final judgment when the evil were separated from the good and is a notion common to many religions: but it was the doom or judgment meted out to the wicked which finally coloured the word.

Now, we know that Anglo-Saxon writers such as Archbishop Wulfstan of York believed in a doom which was felt to be imminent round about AD 1000, that is, a millennium after Christ's birth or death. Wulfstan's cry that the world was coming to an end has already been quoted. To show how common such a belief was I may note its being mentioned in Old English charters dated AD 929, 963, and 987; in the *Blickling Homilies* X and XI (the latter of which was written in 971); and very frequently in the writings of Ælfric. Nor was the belief held only in England: it was well attested on the Continent.

114 A four-drachm piece struck at Alexandria in the year AD 139, the second year of the reign of Antoninus Pius (*LB*), with the word *αιων* to commemorate the start of a new 'æon' or Sothic Cycle. The nimbate Phoenix (Numidian crane) represents the birth of a new era from the ashes of the old.

As far as the peoples of Europe were concerned, they seem to have derived this concept of a cycle of creation and destruction from the East. Although the Hellenistic mystery religions, the cults of Attis, Isis, Osiris and Mithras began as gross and fetichistic nature religions, they developed into faiths in which the primitive elements were gradually spiritualized. From being mere agrarian cults they developed into religions promising deliverance. In a time of decadence, scepticism and mysticism, that is to say round about the Birth of Christ, they attracted large followings by their gorgeous ritual, the magic spell of their Mysteries, their demand for an ascetic life, the blissfulness of the ecstatic state and their promise of salvation and immortality. The devotees of these mystery religions believed that the life of the universe unrolled in a series of 'great years' or world periods, called in Greek *aiones*. When such an aeon reaches   *114*
ripeness there appears the deliverer, the saviour who redeems himself and all mankind from the dominion of the material world. The ascension of this saviour into 'heaven' is the signal for the dissolution of the present aeon. The world passes away in a welter of fire and flood only to rise again fresh and new from its ashes.

The North West European offshoots who had wandered southwards even as far as the shores of the Black Sea fell under the spell of these conceptions, which obtained so strong a hold that (as we have seen) the central figure, the 'Lord' modified in various ways, became known even to the Western branch (our forefathers) and certainly to the Northmen. Thus Balder develops from being a mere fertility god until he occupies the central place in all that happens in the cosmos. This is the view of the world given in the greatest remaining alliterative poem of the North West European peoples, *Völuspá* which, broken and inspissated with darkness as it is, describes sublimely the course of a world period, an aeon extending from the creation of the world to its destruction and the rise of a new earth. This poem is the product of a thousand years and carries us back to the time of the Migration of the Nations.

If we accept the interpretation of the *Dream of the Rood* which I have put forward, then we may believe that the Old English knew something of the world period, 'the great year'. Wulfstan's sermon and other writings of the time tend to confirm such a finding. But we may be sceptical of our ancestors ever having believed in a Ragnarök. On examination this conception proves to have grown by a process of agglutination: it is made up of a number of myths stuck together. The Ragnarök had two fundamental ideas: first, the destruction of the Divine Powers by the sons of Muspell; and second, the assisting of the Divine Powers by warriors who got to heaven by dying honourably on the battlefield. But as I have pointed out, the everlasting battle from which the concept grew already existed in a detached form not only in North West European but also in Celtic myth; and the destruction of Odinn in a wolf's swallow and of Tyr similarly are one and the same myth going back to Indo-European times and telling of a temporary disappearance of the god. The Ragnarök then breaks down into (1) the temporary disappearance of the Sky Father (Odinn, Tyr), (2) the temporary disappearance of the 'Lord' into the Underworld (Balder, Frey), (3) the Everlasting Battle (the Einheriar), (4) the Wild Hunt (Odinn, Valkyries), (5) a deluge myth, and (6) a fire myth. Some, probably all, of these myths were known to the Old English as separate entities: they knew of the temporary disappearance of the Sky Father and of Balder and Frey (Ing), they knew of the Wild Hunt and of the deluge; but there is nowhere any indication that they knew of a synthesized version in which all together had been worked up into a Doom of the Divine Powers.

To summarize the main points of similarity and difference between the Old Norse and Old English myth as I see it: both knew the Sky Father and both saw him change his position with, and lose his wife to, an upstart Wodenaz who became Odinn in the one case and Woden in the other. The Sky Father was relegated to the position of a war god as Tyr or Tiw. Wodenaz retained his two original attributes as god of the dead and a god of magical wisdom in both mythologies; but Odinn, unlike Woden, was developed by Norse poets into the princely host of Valhalla who received as welcome guests all those honourably slain on the battlefield.

Other gods and goddesses were common to Old Norse and Old English peoples as, for instance, Thor-Thunor. Both peoples accepted the Nerthus cult but with minor variations: the representatives of this cult in both schemes were Frig, Freya, Frey-Ing and Balder. Another common concept was that of an all-powerful Fate, Urdr or Wyrd. A host of supernatural beings, giants, dwarfs, elves and nixies were known to both.

As regards the geography of the universe, both Northmen and Englishmen knew of many worlds – seven or nine – supported by a World Tree or pillar, an Yggdrasill or an Irminsul. The earth was the middle enclosure with heaven above and hell beneath. Surrounding the earth was the sea in which lay the Great Serpent holding its tail in its mouth. On the outer shore of the sea there ranged the mountain fells of Giantland.

Each people knew of the concept of the 'great year' with its cycle of creation and destruction; but whereas the Northmen of the Viking Age moulded the destruction after the pattern of their piratical lives and brought it to a final annihilation of world, gods and men, so that the resurrection was entirely forgotten or minimized to such an extent as to lose all meaning, the Old English had long before this become Christian and did not develop a Ragnarök. In fact, after two centuries of fairly peaceful development of the country they had invaded, it is quite certain that far from accepting a Doom of the Divine Powers, the Old English were content merely to replace the old gods by a Prince of Peace who, after all, was for them only an extension of Balder.

115 The 'Lord and Lady' in a Neolithic grave? Skeletons of an old woman, right, and a young man of the Cro-Magnon race from the Grimaldi caves of Barma Grand, Mentone. There is no distinction between the 'solicitude and honour' accorded to the two bodies, unless the head-dressing (a cap of cowrie shells) and superior position of the 'Lady' should indicate a precedence for her.

Chapter Twelve

BALDER INTO CHRIST

The comparatively recent regard for the importance of myths has led to their being translated from the nursery to the study. While they were in the nursery, we regarded myths as fairy-tales; in the study we have come to realize that they are something quite different. But to our ancestors, myths were never fairy-tales, they were the equivalent of what we call scientific truths, being the conclusions they had come to in striving to explain the universe. Modern scientific thought takes individual phenomena and synthesizes them into typical events subject to universal laws. To the scientist, for instance, a chair leg is not just a chair leg but matter made up of galaxies of atoms revolving ceaselessly about one another. Such a conception indicates the great gulf between what we see with our eyes and what science has come to tell us is the 'truth'. Even if I personally am unable to prove such an outlandish scientific truth, nevertheless I accept it because I know that it can be proved to have a greater degree of objectivity than a mere sense impression. But for our Old English forebears the perception of natural phenomena was immediate; they did not translate such perceptions as we may do into conceptions which agree with universal laws. Like all primitive peoples (whether ancient or modern), the pagan Old English looked on natural phenomena as a 'thou' and not an 'it'. Their approach to nature was subjective as opposed to the scientist's objectivity. In interpreting natural phenomena they were intuitive rather than rational and so their interpretation of the universe is by revelation which assumes form and body in myth. It is not to be wondered at that the myths of all primitive peoples are couched in verse, for poets were the instruments of the revelation: poets were the scientists of the ancient world and in the new scientific view of the universe there is, alas, no place for them.

Because of the immediacy of their apprehension of natural phenomena, divine and demonic powers were for the Old English immanent in Nature. This feeling of the immanence of divinity was shared by all primitive peoples except one whom I will mention in a moment; and because these primitives regarded natural phenomena basically in the same light we find a striking similarity in their myths. If, for example, we compare our North West European forefathers' interpretation with that of ancient Egyptians and Sumerians we find the three chief deities given embodiment in the Sky, Air and Earth as the following table shows:

	Sumerians	Egyptians	N. W. Europeans
Sky	Anu	Nut	Tiwaz
Air	Enlil	Shu	Wodenaz
Earth	Ninlil	Geb	Nerthus

But there was one people who did *not* see god as immanent in nature but as *transcending* nature – the Hebrews. To the Hebrews their god Yahweh or Jehovah was not in nature: for them sky, air and earth were not divine, but natural phenomena which were reflections of a God whom it was not even possible properly to name:

> And, behold, the LORD passed by, and a great and strong wind rent the mountains, and brake in pieces the rocks before the LORD; but the LORD was not in the wind: and after the wind an earthquake; but the LORD was not in the earthquake: and after the earthquake a fire; but the LORD was not in the fire: and after the fire a still small voice. (I Kings 19. 11–12.)
>
> And God said unto Moses: I AM THAT I AM: and he said, Thus shalt thou say unto the children of Israel, I AM hath sent me unto you. (Exodus 3. 14.)

The God of the Hebrews is pure being, unqualified and ineffable.

Now, we have to remember that the religion which swept across Europe from the first century of this era was not Hebraism but Christianity, and whichever way we look at it the Christian myth is basically the Near Eastern myth of the 'Lord': for 'Our Lord' Jesus is the son of the virgin mother who dies into the Underworld and who is resurrected significantly at Easter, the spring of the year. It is immaterial whether we regard Jesus the son of Mary as historical or not: the account of his life, death and resurrection as told in the Gospels is still the story of the 'Lord'. And what it is important to realize is that the mass of Christian converts (in Europe at least) who had previously subscribed to cults where god was immanent in nature could and still did believe in this immanence. One thing is certain, Jesus can never be claimed to be like Jehovah transcendent, pure being, unqualified, ineffable.

How and why did our forefathers come to take to Christianity? To attempt to answer this question we need to dig deep. First we may take note of a significant difference in ancient times between the Indo-European peoples and some of those of the eastern Mediterranean seaboard in the way in which their societies were organized. The basis of Indo-European society was in general the father and his authority; of Mediterranean society, the mother and her authority. As we have seen, this state of affairs came to be reflected in the religious attitude of the two divisions of peoples, in the one the chief divinity comes to be a Sky Father, in the other an Earth Mother.

Confining the discussion to our ancestors of the Indo-European complex, the North West Europeans, we see during the last two thousand years an outward maintenance of the superiority of the male. We may

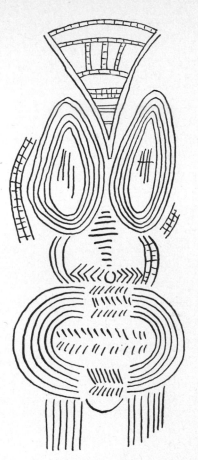

116, 117 A fossilized mammoth tusk from the
Gravettian site of Předmost, Czechoslovakia,
engraved with the stylized representation of a
woman. The drawing is not a realistic portrait of a
woman, it is rather a map or key to what the artist
regarded as quintessential feminity.

suspect that that superiority has fairly recently been impaired by the emancipation of women in Western Europe and by the powerful position in society achieved by the women of the USA, a country, one might have the temerity to say, where women appear to be regaining their natural position.

My contention (outlandish as it may seem) is that the female was originally the superior sex by reason of being the *only* sex. When the first protozoic female atom of life-slime reproduced itself partheno-genetically as usual but, as a precedent brought forth a new sex, male, it took the first fatal step towards undermining its own authority. From that day, millions of years ago, to this, the myth of the superiority of the male has grown and flourished. For instead of retaining her power of reproducing life on her own, the female had now delegated half of that power to the male: as far as Man was concerned, neither sex was fully capable of creating life, and the female primeval urge to give birth would in its need for fulfilment, eventually lead the sex to surrender to the male.

It is a mistake to believe (arguing now only about men and women), that man is the stronger of the two. Individually, men may be stronger than women, but inherently woman is really the stronger. We have only to study our vital statistics to acknowledge this. Individual men may run faster, swim longer, lift heavier weights, but this is merely because they have neither the fundamental urge nor the mechanics to deploy their strength in the essentials of life (if life is to go on), such as menstruation, gestation, parturition and lactation.

It is informative to consider in what regard women were held in pre-history – at the dawn of time. Typical burials of the finest type of Neo-anthropics, the New Men who came after the Neanderthalers, such as those in the cave of Barma Grand, Mentone, show no distinction between the solicitude and honour accorded to men and women. There is no sign of the subjection of women until we reach more 'civilized' times. On the contrary, among the Neoanthropics woman was singled out for special attention. Dating from these remote ages are the diagrammatic drawings and sculptures which emphasize the essential qualities of women such as the drawing from Předmost and the statuette from Willendorf. The Předmost diagram can never be claimed to be realistic – it is rather a chart or map of quintessential femininity (according to the ideas of early man), such as a modern painter like Picasso might attempt; nor can the more realistic 'Venus' of Willendorf be claimed to be a truthful portrait of Palaeolithic Woman. The artist had a motive for carving what almost amounts to a caricature, and that motive is to be found in the grotesque emphasis given to the distinguishing female physical traits – those traits which when exaggerated turn a statue of a woman into a symbol of fertility, namely the capacious belly which is the repository of the new life, the open vulva from which it emerges and the bounteous breasts which nourish it. Perhaps it is too much to claim that these female figurines (found, as they are, from Britain to India) were intended to be representations of the Great Goddess, Earth Mother; but they must represent the archetype out of which the conception grew.

115

116, 117

118

119–121

118 The 'Venus' of Willendorf, a Gravettian figurine found at Willendorf in Austria. Such representations of the female figure are significant in displaying not a true-to-life portrait but in concentrating on those physical features of the female body which, when exaggerated, turn a statue of a woman into a symbol of fertility.

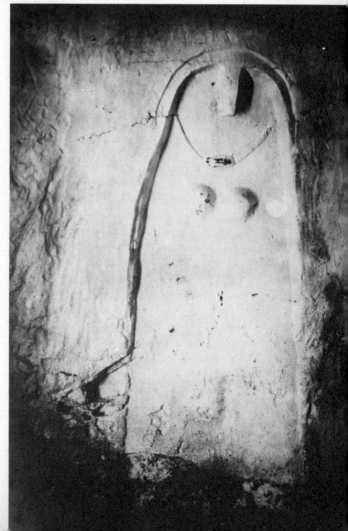

119–121 Woman as the supreme fertility
figure, progenitor of the human race, is
depicted in figurines found from Europe to
India. The chalk 'goddess' (*top left*) from the
flint-mines at Grimes Graves, Norfolk, was
discovered on a small altar in an abandoned
working; she is typical in having the
exaggerated physical characteristics associated
with fertility. The Neolithic 'goddess' (*left*)
from Croizard, Marne, not only has the usual
stylized female features but also wears a
necklace, later to become one of the personal
attributes of the 'Lady' (Ill. 78). An excess of
jewellery (including once more the necklace)
on the clay figurine (*above*) from Sari Dehri,
India (second millennium BC) nevertheless,
does not obscure the prominent sexual
characteristic of these 'Venus' figurines.

122 Palaeolithic scene from the 'Shaft of the Dead Man' at Lascaux. A realistic representation of a dead bison and the man killed by it. There is no fertility element here, for the erect penis could well have been seen by the artist – a consequence of the man's back being broken.

There are in existence, too, contemporary depictions of Palaeolithic men, but the important thing to notice is that these representations are attempts to reproduce realistic portraits. They are not exaggerated as the female figurines are. It is only later that the male form comes to be exaggerated: then, attention is centred on the male generative organ and we see the beginning of the representation of penises much larger than life. There can be only one explanation of this phallic development coming later than that of the female figurines: it was only later on that man came to realize his own part in the procreation of children.

In primitive societies where men have come to understand the part they play in conception, man has asserted a superiority based on his being an essential link in the chain of reproduction; but occasionally, in other societies just as primitive (like the Trobrianders), where no man ever knew he was a father, the ancient order has prevailed and woman has retained her superior position. We have seen the two opposing types of society in the patriarchal Indo-Europeans and the matriarchal Mediterranean peoples.

Nevertheless, all normal men and women know intuitively about their primeval relationship. This intuitive knowledge finds expression (I contend) in the instinctive urge of the female to envelop the male, to achieve unity with him in coition and so become complete again; just as the instinctive urge of the male is to penetrate and be lost in the female. It is only those fortunate men and women who at times are able to experience this mystical one-ness who have in this respect achieved for a few fleeting seconds the original sex-less state.

My belief is that societies have in the past been influenced by this intuitive knowledge of the primeval relationship between male and female and this has resulted in their arranging themselves as a matriarchal society. Often enough patriarchal societies have organized themselves *partly* as matriarchies, especially where religion is concerned. We see this in Europe and the West today in those countries where Roman Catholicism still has a hold. The 'Great Goddess', the Virgin Mother, *123, 124* has succeeded in the person of Mary in re-establishing her position among many Eastern and Western Christians. If we look at her historical development, we see that at first the Virgin was neglected, but from the fourth century onwards there is a marked growth in the devotion accorded by Christians to Mary. In the early part of the fifth century Nestorius objected to Mary's being called *Theotokos* 'Mother of God', but in AD 431 the Council of Ephesus confirmed the title – a fitting place for this confirmation when we remember Diana the tutelary deity of the Ephesians. Regard for Mary has grown by leaps and bounds, enough to overshadow the devotion accorded to her son Jesus. There has been some hair-splitting: the especial veneration shown to Mary, while sneered at as 'Mariolatry' by some Protestants, is distinguished by Catholic theologians from the supreme adoration due to the Godhead alone. However, when in 1950, Pope Pius XII proclaimed by the bull *Munificentissimus Deus* the dogma of the bodily ascent into heaven of the Virgin Mary, it seemed clear that as far as ordinary Catholics are concerned, the Great Goddess had once more taken up her position of superiority.

Here then in religion, Catholics have accepted what many men accept intuitively. The intuition has changed the social order throughout history. It was thwarted in England once, by one man, King Henry VIII who, ironically enough, in the urge to subdue himself to the eternal female, prevented his new Protestants from doing it in established religion. The intuition was gradually working itself out as far as religion is concerned among the North West Europeans of the first centuries of this era: it was being brought about through the cult of Nerthus which, as we have seen, struggled to assert itself among our own direct ancestors as well as among the Northmen. If we look at the change wrought among the Northmen we find the first hostile reaction of a patriarchal society was to alter the sex of the Great Goddess so that female Nerthus became male Niord: but the virgin's son reappears in the person of Frey, and as Niord withdraws into the background, the Great Goddess reasserts herself as Freya. In Sweden one might say the process had almost completed itself by AD 1000.

123, 124 The basic iconography of the Lady goddess and her son as depicted in the bronze Egyptian statuette of Isis and Horus (*right*), and in the Coptic wall-painting (*above*) of Mary and Jesus from the Monastery of St Jeremias, Saqqara (sixth–seventh century).

In the north, too, there was the parallel figure to Frey or Balder with the Great Goddess either as his wife Nanna or his mother Frig. Norse poets allowed environment to overcome intuition as far as Balder was concerned by turning him into the supreme Viking and fitting him into their nihilistic concept of the destruction of everything: his death became the most important thing about him as the presager of the Ragnarök. The Great Goddess (his wife or mother) was relegated to the normal place occupied by women in a patriarchal society, that is to say inferior to the male. This was the position at the latest by the time the *Edda* poems were being composed, namely about A D 800.

As for the Old English, they had subscribed to the cult of the Great Goddess as Nerthus while on the Continent; in Britain they continued to venerate the persons of the cult as 'Mother Earth', Frig, Freya, Frey-Ing and Balder. As we have noticed from the *Dream of the Rood*, the memory of Balder was strong after the conversion of the English to Christianity. And this might well be, for what had happened but one thing? The cult of the Great Goddess had worked its way west at first in our ancestors' baggage in their own version where the personages are Mother Earth, Frig, Freya, Frey and Balder, only to be joined in A D 597 by the Italian missionary version in which the persons are called Mary and Jesus.

In adopting the Christian religion what exactly were the Northmen and our own Old English forebears doing? For the ordinary folk of both branches of the North West European race Christianity did not mean anything like what it has come to mean in later centuries – the Thirty-nine Articles or the Pauline doctrine or even the tenets of the Sermon on the Mount. It meant a story of a child born miraculously of a virgin mother, born in the dead of winter, surrounded significantly by the beasts of the field, the ox and the ass with the sheep and shepherd hard by on the frosty hill. It is the story of a baby whose birth was mystically connected with a time of peace over the whole earth, who grew to manhood, suffered a bloody wound and died to be resurrected again from the dead. And perhaps most important, the death and resurrection of Jesus was a necessity that the world might live. This was what the 'new' story, the 'new' myth, the 'new' religion meant to the ordinary people, and it was compatible with many fertility rites and observances such as the blessing of the plough, of rivers and the sea, with conjuration of fruit trees, with prayers for good seasons, rain and the general fertility of the earth, with thanksgiving at harvest, with mourning and rejoicing at Easter for the death of the god and his resurrection.

Today, organized Christianity is dying a lingering death, smothered under an accretion of man-made dogma and doctrine which is vainly invoked to answer the scientist who (if the truth be known) looks like hoisting himself with his own petard anyway in the shape of the hydrogen bomb: it is only at the main festivals, Christmas and Easter, the birth and the death and rebirth of God, that its adherents show any sign of real religious activity. For the modern Christ has been crucified on the wheels of industry created by science and his body buried under a slagheap from whose smoky and infertile clinker no growth comes, no resurrection can be expected. What the Northmen were unable to achieve in their Ragnarök, namely to keep under the god of fertility, we moderns, children of Science and the Industrial Revolution, have succeeded in doing.

This is the lesson to be learnt from a study of Wayland's Bones, that man needs to integrate himself with Nature: for ultimately the Great Goddess *is* Nature from whom all life proceeds and to whom it will return. I am not suggesting a wholesale march back to Eden, for Town-Man has shut himself off from the earth by concrete and tarmacadam, from the sky by bricks and slate, and has accepted the rule of the clock which will not be put back. Nor am I suggesting that the outward manifestations of Nature are immutable, for they are not: the development of Man himself has shown the changeableness of Nature's forms. But if the aim is freedom from the bodily and mental ills modern Man has largely brought upon himself, freedom from illness and *angst*, then those individuals who take practical steps to make their peace with Nature in what they eat and drink, in how they think, sleep and behave – these peace-makers shall inherit the earth. In effect, we have to stop regarding ourselves as things apart – Man as opposed to animals and plants, or Man in vacuous space without what the botanists call a habitat. We have to reach a symbiotic relationship with all else in the world, living or dead. No doubt some such was the aim of our ancestors and we may be wise to ponder on how they attempted to reach it.

LIST OF ILLUSTRATIONS

26 Anglo-Saxon bronze girdle-hooks from Soham, Cambs. British Museum. Photo courtesy of the Trustees of the British Museum.

27 The Roman Baths, Bath. Photo Peter Clayton.

28 Map of the Saxon Shore forts in the *Notitia Dignitatum*, 436. Bodleian Library, Oxford. Photo Oxford University Press.

29 Christ-Helios mosaic beneath the Vatican, Rome. Photo Fototeca Unione.

30 Aerial view of the Wansdyke in Wiltshire. Copyright reserved, Director of Aerial Photography, University of Cambridge.

31 Grimsdyke, near Downton, Wilts. Copyright reserved, Director of Aerial Photography, University of Cambridge.

32 Vale of Pewsey with the White Horse. Photo Peter Clayton.

33 Utrecht Psalter, fol. 22r. Harley MS. 603. British Museum. Photo courtesy of the Trustees of the British Museum.

34 Pagan Anglo-Saxon jewellery. British Museum. Photo Peter Davey.

35 Anglo-Saxon jewellery of the seventh to tenth centuries. British Museum. Photo John Webb, Brompton Studios.

36 *Lacnunga* charm MS. Harley MS. 585. British Museum. Photo courtesy of the Trustees of the British Museum.

37 Utrecht Psalter, fol. 54v. Harley MS. 603. British Museum. Photo courtesy of the Trustees of the British Museum.

38 *Waldere* MS. Kongelige Bibliotek, Copenhagen. Photo courtesy of the Librarian.

39 The Sutton Hoo lyre. British Museum. Photo courtesy of the Trustees of the British Museum.

40 *Beowulf* MS. British Museum. Photo courtesy of the Trustees of the British Museum.

41 Fifteenth-century barn, Place Farm, Tisbury, Wilts. Photo Edwin Smith.

42 Engraving of the three Weird Sisters. Holinshed's *Chronicles*, first edition, 1577. Photo Ray Gardner.

43 Purse-top and clasps from Sutton Hoo. British Museum. Photo John Webb, Brompton Studios.

44 'Sun-chariot' from Trundholm. National Museum, Copenhagen. Museum photo.

45 Samson. Fifteenth-century Book of Drawings, Arnamagean Collection, Copenhagen, no. 673 a III.

46 Aerial view of the Sutton Hoo cemetery. Copyright reserved, Director of Aerial Photography, University of Cambridge.

47 Impression of the ship found at Sutton Hoo. Photo courtesy of the Trustees of the British Museum.

48 Professor Stuart Piggott's drawing of the Sutton Hoo deposit. Photo courtesy of the Trustees of the British Museum.

49 Ceremonial whetstone from Sutton Hoo. British Museum. Photo courtesy of the Trustees of the British Museum.

50 Iron standard from Sutton Hoo. British Museum. Photo courtesy of the Trustees of the British Museum.

51 Sutton Hoo helmet. British Museum. Photo courtesy of the Trustees of the British Museum.

52 Helmet plaque from the Sutton Hoo helmet. British Museum. Photo courtesy of the Trustees of the British Museum.

53 Bronze die for embossing helmet plates from Torslunda, Sweden. Statens Historiska Museum, Stockholm. Photo ATA, Stockholm.

54 Coins from the Sutton Hoo purse. British Museum. Photo Peter Clayton.

55 Detail of the Sutton Hoo purse-top. British Museum. Photo courtesy of the Trustees of the British Museum.

56 Bronze die for embossing helmet plates, from Torslunda, Sweden. Photo courtesy of the Statens Historiska Museum, Stockholm.

57 Silver plate from Sutton Hoo. British Museum. Photo courtesy of the Trustees of the British Museum.

58 Hanged man. Jónsbók, sixteenth century. Arnamagnean Collection, Copenhagen, no. 345.

59 Gravestone from Tjängride, Gothland. Photo ATA, Stockholm.

60 Utrecht Psalter, fol. lv. Harley MS. 603. British Museum. Photo courtesy of the Trustees of the British Museum.

61 Tollund Man. Silkeborg Museum. Photo Niels Elsing, Danish National Museum.

62 The Windeby girl. Schloss Gothorp, Schleswig-Holsteinisches Landesmuseum. Museum photo.

63 Piersbridge altar to Jupiter Dolichenus. After Haverfield's drawing, courtesy of the Chapter Librarian, Durham Cathedral.

64 Jupiter Dolichenus. Capitoline Museum, Rome. Museum photo.

65 Hittite weather god, from Zingirli, North Syria. Ankara Museum. Photo Max Hirmer.

66 Sword-chape from Thorsbjaerg bog. National Museum, Copenhagen. Museum photo.

67 Painting of Uppsala by C.J. Billmark. Photo ATA, Stockholm.

68 Hittite relief from Malatya. Ankara Museum. Photo Josephine Powell.

69 Detail of the Gosforth Cross, Cumberland. Photo B.T. Batsford, courtesy of the Royal Commission on Historical Monuments (England).

70 Carved slab. Gosforth Church, Cumberland. Photo B.T. Batsford, courtesy of the Royal Commission on Historical Monuments (England).

71 Memorial stone, Altuna, Sweden. Photo courtesy of the Statens Historiska Museum, Stockholm.

72 Seventeenth-century painting of the World Serpent. Arnamagnean Collection, Copenhagen, no. 738.

73 Anglo-Saxon cross-head. Chapter House, Durham Cathedral. Photo courtesy of the Dean and Chapter of Durham.

74 Panel from the lid of the Franks Casket. British Museum. Photo courtesy of the Trustees of the British Museum.

75 Gold *labrys*. Herakleion Museum. Photo Peter Clayton.

76 Cart from the Oseberg ship. Universitetets Oldsaksamling, Oslo.

77 Detail from cart found in the Oseberg ship. Universitetets Oldsaksamling, Oslo.

78 Rynkeby Cauldron. Danish National Museum, Copenhagen. Photo Niels Elswing.

79 Ishtar figures on a Cypriot sarcophagus. Metropolitan Museum of Art, New York.

80 Votive tablet from Locri. Reggio Museum. Photo Soprintendenza alle Antichità, Reggio di Calabria.

81 Temple of Demeter at Eleusis. Photo Max Hirmer.

82 Freya figure from Rebild Skovmose. Danish National Museum, Copenhagen. Photo courtesy of Professor P.V. Glob.

83 Bronze Age wagon from Dejbjerg. Danish National Museum, Copenhagen. Photo Niels Elswing.

84 Iron helmet from Grave I, Vendel. Statens Historiska Museum, Stockholm. Photo ATA, Stockholm.

85 Wooden male figure from Broddenbjerg. Danish National Museum, Copenhagen. Museum photo.

86 Gold plaques from Jäderen. Historisk Museum, Bergen, Norway.

87 Hermod rides to Hel. Eighteenth-century manuscript of the *Snorra Edda*. Royal Library, Copenhagen, New collection no. 1867

88 Cuneiform tablet K162. British Museum. Photo courtesy of the Trustees of the British Museum.

89 Cylinder-seal impression showing Ishtar. Oriental Institute, University of Chicago.

90 'Goddess of Animals', agate gem from Mycenae. Photo Peter Clayton, after Evans.

91 'Master of Animals', gem from Canea, Kydonia. Photo Peter Clayton, after Evans.

92 Roman silver plate. Castello Sforzesco, Milan. Photo Max Hirmer.

93 Benty Grange helmet. Sheffield Museum. Photo British Museum Laboratory.

94 Boar crest on the Benty Grange helmet. Sheffield Museum. Museum photo.

95 Detail of Sutton Hoo clasp. British Museum. Photo courtesy of the Trustees of the British Museum.

96 Bronze die for embossing helmet plates from Torslunda. Statens Historiska Museum, Stockholm. Photo ATA, Stockholm.

97 Sheela-na-gig with animal supporter. Whittlesford Church, Cambridgeshire. Photo author.

98 Sheela-na-gig. Kilpeck Church, Herefordshire. Photo Malcolm Thurlby.

99, 100 Wooden 'sprouting' Osiris figure from the tomb of Tutankhamun, Thebes. Cairo Museum. Photos courtesy of the Griffith Institute, Ashmolean Museum, Oxford.

101 *Völuspá*, fol. 2r. National Library, Reykjavik, Iceland.

102 Carved panel from Bjarnastadahlid, Skagafjördur. National Museum of Iceland, Reykjavik. Photo Giseli Gestsson.

103 *Dream of the Rood* manuscript. Vercelli Cathedral Library, MS. CXVII, fol. 104v. Photo courtesy of the Librarian, Vercelli Cathedral.

104 Runes on the Ruthwell Cross. Drawn by the author.

105 Ruthwell Cross, Dumfriesshire. Photo Warburg Institute, London.

106 Page from the *Völuspá* MS. fol. 2v. National Library, Reykjavik, Iceland.

107 Engraving of the temple at Uppsala by Olaus Magnus, 1555. Photo ATA, Stockholm.

108 Detail of the Gundestrup cauldron. Danish National Museum, Copenhagen. Museum photo.

109 Greenfield Papyrus (BM 10554; 87). British Museum. Photo John Webb, Brompton Studios.

110 Interior of sarcophagus lid of Ankh-nes-nefer-ib-re. British Museum. Photo courtesy of the Trustees of the British Museum.

111 Maypole before St Andrew Undershaft, from the *Penny Magazine*. Photo R. B. Fleming Ltd.

112 Cædmon's *Genesis* manuscript. Bodleian Library, Oxford, MS. Junius II, P66.

113 Gylfi before Odinn. *Snorra Edda*, fourteenth century. University Library, Uppsala. Delagardie, no. 11.

114 Billon tetradrachm of Antoninus Pius struck at Alexandria. Photo Peter Clayton.

115 Neanderthal skeletons from the Barma Grand, Grimaldi cave, Monaco. Photo British Museum (Natural History).

116, 117 Venus of Předmost. Archaeological Institute of the Czechoslovakian Academy of Sciences. Photo J. Kleibl.

118 Venus of Willendorf. Photo Peter Clayton.

119 Chalk 'goddess' from Grimes Graves, Norfolk. British Museum. Photo courtesy of the Trustees of the British Museum.

120 Female representation, Croizard, Marne. Photo Musée de l'Homme, Paris.

121 Female figurine from Sari Dehri, India. Boston Museum of Fine Arts. Museum photo.

122 'Shaft of the Dead Man', Lascaux, France. Photo Archives Photographiques.

123 Coptic wall-painting of Mary and Jesus, Saqqara. Photo Service des Antiquités, Egypt.

124 Isis and Horus. Private collection. Photo courtesy of the Trustees of the British Museum.

INDEX

Illustration numbers are given in italic

ADAM OF BREMEN, and temple at
Uppsala 114 f., 139, 176; *107*
Adonis 35, 139, 155, 164; his myth
158; relationship to Balder 162
Ægir, sea god before Niord 135 f.
Æsir, the Norse gods, shackle Fenrir
80, 135; their home 145, 173ff.
Albin, J., on Sheela-na-gig at Bin-
stead, I.O.W. 154 f.
Alföðr 76, 183
Alfred 22, 67; and Treaty of Wed-
more 120
Allfather, as the ancient Sky Father
76ff., 171, 183; and myth of Night
and Day 78
America, and the Vikings 115 f.
Angles 7, 15, 19, 23, 28, 31, 33, 35, 55,
57, 58, 64, 93, 135, 178
Angli 128 f., 135
Anglo-Saxon Chronicle, and Sceaf 18;
Wild Hunt 94; human sacrifice 104
Annarr, byname for Odinn 77
Anu, Sumerian Sky God 190
Asgard, Norse heaven 76; and *Beo-
wulf* 145; *113*
Attis 35, 139, 155, 185
Audience of Beowulf, and Flood 47
Augustine, mission to England 35,
53, 57 f.
Aurgelmir, or Ymir 172, 178
axe, double- 110, 113

BAAL 131, 155
Balder 49, 139; killed by Höder and
Loki 134, 173; the Bleeding God
157 ff.; and cult of the 'Lord' 185 ff.;
87, 101, 103, 104, 105

barn, at Tisbury *41*, *v*. also *24*
Bath, Roman ruins *27*
Beadohild, her story in Anglo-Saxon
Deor's Lament 8, 12
Bede 22; describes Old English
paganism 51 ff.
Beowulf 28; fights Grendel 62 f.;
given boar's-head standard 151
Beowulf, Anglo-Saxon epic poem,
and Wayland 8, 12; Scyld Scefing
18, his burial 90 f.; Heorot 31;
giants overwhelmed in Flood 43,
46ff., 177; harping 59; outline
story 62 f.; Scandinavian history
64; 'wyrd' 65 ff.; 'frea' meaning
'lord' 139; Brosingamen 143 f.;
boar images 151; *bealdor* meaning
'lord' 157; *eci dryctin* 183; ship
grave *16*; manuscript *40*; hall *41*;
helmet *51–53, 84, 93, 94*
Bergelmir, giant who escapes Flood
48, 172
Bifröst, rainbow bridge 145, 175
Bleeding God 157 ff.
Blotmonath 52
boars 151; on Sutton Hoo clasps *43,
95*
Bodvild (Anglo-Saxon Beadohild),
her story in Norse *Lay of Volund*
12 ff.
body, preserved in Danish bog *62*, *v*.
also *61*
Boniface 28, 54, 116
Brisingamen 143, 149
Brosingamen 143
bucket from Sutton Hoo ship burial
19
Burgh Castle 7, *9*

209

CAEDMON, and Creation 180f.
cart, v. wagon
Catholic(s) 55; 'Great Goddess', i.e.
Mary 197
Celts 15, 109ff., 126
Ceres 117
Charlemagne, destroys Irminsul
175f.
Charms; demonstrate pagan beliefs
49ff.; remember marriage of Earth
Mother and Sky Father 77, 128,
143; Valkyries 106; Longeus the
blind legionary 169; page from
Lucnunga 36
Chaucer, refers to Wayland's father
8; Fates 67
Christ, on Frank's Casket 9, 15;
struggles against Near East fertility
gods 35, 101; accepted alongside
pagan deities 54, 116; the 'young
hero' 60; subject to Fate 65, 126,
128, 131; Frey identified with 139,
143, 154; Dream of the Rood 165ff.;
Balder identified with 189ff.;
Christ-Helios 29
Christianity 28, 47, 54, 64, 79, 190,
200; adopts pagan ideas 35, 38;
Old English converted to 57ff., 66;
and Sheela-na-gig 152f.; Icelanders converted to 171
Church, Christian, 7f., 35, 38, 58, 67,
127
Count of the Saxon Shore, Roman
coastal commander 23; his forts
7–9, 28
Creation Myth, North West European 49, Anglo-Saxon 180f., 183
Crucifixion, in Dream of the Rood 65,
168; Odinn's 97f.
Cybele, Earth Mother 92

DANIEL motif 88
Deivos, Indo-European Sky Father
72
Demeter, Greek goddess, temple at
Eleusis 80
Deor's Lament, and story of Wayland
8, 12
Destiny, or Wyrd 58, 64
Divine Family 72
Djevs, Indo-European Sky Father
72f., 77, 109, 127

doom 183 ff.
Doom of the Divine Powers 79ff.,
122, 162f., 169f., 186
Doom of the Gods 100, 140, 162, 164
Dream of the Rood 60, 65, 186; Frey in
139, 143; Balder in 165, 200;
quoted in runes on Ruthwell Cross
165ff.; 103–105
dwarfs 174, 186; support the heavens
172, 176
Dyaus, Hindu Sky Father 74, 112, 128
Dyauspitar, Hindu Sky Father 74

EARENDEL, O. Icelandic Orvandill
126
Earth Mother goddess, 50, 52f., 55,
190; daughter of Annarr 77; married to Sky Father 77; mother of
Thunor 113, 120; as Fiörgynn,
Jorth and Nerthus 127ff., 152f.,
172; and lost lover 143, 145, 149;
figurines of 196; in Denmark 78, v.
also 76, 77, 92
Egil the archer, on Franks Casket 126,
74
Einheriar, Chosen Slain in Valhalla
99f., 186
elf shot, man molested by 33
elves 46f., 174f., 186
Enlil, Sumerian Air God 190
Eostre, Anglo-Saxon Goddess 51, 128
Everlasting Battle 186

FATAL Sisters, and Wyrd 66; poem by
John Gray 101
Fate, Anglo-Saxon belief in 46, 64ff.;
Odinn at the mercy of 76, 173; all-
powerful 186
female figurines 192f., 119–121, v.
also 122
Fenrir or Fenriswulf, monstrous wolf
shackled in the Underworld 80;
swallows Odinn 82
Fiörgynn (1) weather god supplanted
by Thunor 113
(2) father of Frig 127
fivefold kiss, in witchcraft 155
flood, gods overwhelm giants in 43,
177; story in runes on sword 47ff.
Franks Casket, finding of 9; has
scenes of pagan myth 9ff., 62; and
Wayland Smith 48; story of Orvandill 126; 1–4, 5, 74

210

frea, meaning 'lord' 139, 157
Frey, fertility god, as Fricco 114f.; supplants weather god in Sweden 126; as 'Lord' 132ff; and religious prostitution 155, 157; son of Niord 173; in Cædmon's *Hymn* 183; temporary disappearance of 186f.; as 'virgin's son' 197f.; *85*, *86*
Freya, northern Earth Mother 128, 152, 157, 186, 200; as chooser of the slain 100; threatened kidnapping of 123; as Earth Mother 131f., 133ff.; called 'the whore' 155; daughter of Niord 173
Fricco, i.e. Frey 114f., 139
Frig, in English place-names 41f., 127; worshipped in England 55; as Mother Earth 127ff., 186, 200; identified with Freya 136, 149, and myth of Balder's Death 158ff.; Odinn's wife 172

GABRIEL's Hounds 94
gallows, and Odinn 58
Garm, hound guarding Hel, Swallows Sky Father 82, 186
Gerda, and Frey 139ff.; *86*
Germania, and chariot of the sun 78; runes 97; Mother Earth 128f., 151; Tvisto and Creation myth 178
giants 174f.; attack gods and are drowned 43, 46ff.; Frost Giants 82, 173; Ymir 172, 177, 178
girdle hooks *26*
gleewood, Anglo-Saxon lyre 59; from Sutton Hoo ship burial *39*
Goddess of Animals 88; and Sheela-na-gig 155; *90*
Gokstad ship *14*, *15*
Gosforth Church, panel depicting Thunor fishing for the World Serpent 120
Great Goddess, Earth Mother 131f., 192; as Sheela-na-gig 155; and Christianity 197; on votive tablet *81*
Great Rite, ceremonial copulation in modern witchcraft 155
'great years' 185; *114*
Grim, nickname of Woden 41f.
Grimsdyke, Woden's earthwork 42; *31*
Gundestrup cauldron *108*

Gunnar Helming, pretends to be Frey 136f.

HÄGGEBY rock-carved boat *6*
Hammer, of Thunor 53, 117; or *labrys* of Indo-European weather god 113
heathenism 35ff.
Hebraism 190
Heer, das wütende 94
Heimdall, in *Beowulf* 145; at Balder's funeral 161; son of Odinn 172; and Cædmon's *Hymn* 183
Hel (1) goddess of Norse Underworld 134, 159, 161f.; daughter of Loki and Angrboda 173
(2) Old Norse Underworld 164
helmet, from Sutton Hoo 51; from Vendel *84*; with boar crest *93*, *94*, *96*
Hermod, messenger of the gods 159; rides to Hel to ransom Balder 161; son of Odinn 172; *87*
History of the Anglo-Saxons 43, 45, 47
Hittites 17; and weather god 109f., 117f.
Höder, blind god who kills Balder 134, 159, 169; returns from Hel 164; as Roman soldier Longeus 169; son of Odinn 172
Holinshed's *Chronicles* 68ff.
Horus, Egyptian god *123*
house, Anglo-Saxon at Bourton-on-the-Water *24*, *v*. also *23* and *41*
Hrothgar, Danish king in *Beowulf* 28, 59, 62, 151

IDOLS in England 53f.
Illuyankas, Hittite monster 120
Indo-Europeans 16ff., 190; and Creation myth 49, 72ff.; and weather god 109ff., 117f., 126; patriarchal system 129f., 140; Greek branch 151; basic vocabulary 174
Indra, Hindu god doublet of Thor 109f., 117
Ing, Ingi, Yng or Yngvi, a doublet of Frey 138f., 186, 200
Irminsul, a universal column 176f., 187
Ishtar, the Great Goddess 131; journey to the Underground 139, 145ff.; *79*, *88*, *89*

Isis, Egyptian goddess *123*

Wild Hunt 94 f., 107, 186
witchcraft 155
Woden, chief Anglo-Saxon god 41 f., 49, 55, 62; usurps the place of the Sky Father 75, 85 ff., 116; husband of Frig 127, 174, 186; *30–32*
Wodenaz, primitive West European god 93 f.; name related to Latin *vates* 96 f.; usurps place of Sky Father 101 f., 113, 186, 190
Woden's Hunt 94
wolf 80 f., 98, 186; *102*
Wolthuthliwaz 97, 114, 117, 183
World Ash Tree 68, 168; described 175 f., 186 f.; *107, 111*
'world periods', Greek *aiones* or 'Great Years' 185 f.; *114*
World Serpent, Jormungand or Midgard's Worm, Thor fishes for 120 ff., 126; *69–72*
Wuldor 97, 157
Wuldorfæder 114, 117
wuldortanas 97
Wyrd 57 ff., 168, 174, 186

YEAVERING, royal palace *23*, v. also *24, 41*
Yggdrasill, 46, 68 f.; and Mimir 82; Odinn crucified on 98, 168, 172; described 175 f., 187; *107, 111*
Ymir, giant killed by Odinn 47, 172, 177 f.
Yng or Frey 138
Ynglinga saga, describes spread of cult of Wodenaz 104; Odinn's death 135; Frey 139
Yngvi, or Frey 138
Yngvifrey 138
Yule, connection with boar's head and Frey 151

ZEUS 158; Greek Sky God counterpart of Dyaus, Jovis and Tiwaz 72 f., 112; and Erinyes 107; and oak tree 116
Zeuspater, Zeus as father of gods and men 72, 183
Ziu, Germanic form of Tiw and Tyr 72 f.